FEDERICO GARCÍA LORCA

Blood Wedding

translated,
with Commentary and Notes by
GWYNNE EDWARDS

Bloomsbury Methuen Drama
An imprint of Bloomsbury Publishing Plc
BLOOMSBURY
NEW DELHI • LONDON • OXFORD • NEW YORK • SYDNEY

First published in India 2017
This translation first published in Great Britain in 1987 by Methuen London Ltd
First published in Great Britain in this edition in 1997 by
Methuen Drama Reissued with additional material and a new cover design 2006, 2009
Reprinted by Bloomsbury Methuen Drama 2013, 2013, 2014, 2015 (twice), 2016

Photographs are from the 1987 production of
BloodWedding at the Contact Theatre, Manchester
Photographs © Arthur Thompson

British Library Cataloguing-in-Publication Data
A catalogue record for this book is available from the British Library.
Library of Congress Cataloging-in-Publication Data
A catalog record for this book is available from the Library of Congress.

ISBN: 978 93 86349 28 6

For sale in the Indian subcontinent only

Bloomsbury Publishing India Pvt. Ltd
Second Floor, Building No. 4
DDA Complex LSC, Pocket C – 6 & 7
Vasant Kunj, New Delhi 110070
www.bloomsbury.com

Series: Student Editions
Printed at Manipal Technologies Limited, Manipal

Contents

Federico García Lorca: 1898–1936 v

Plot xi

Commentary
- Lorca and the theatre of his time xvi
- Staging of Lorca's plays in his lifetime xxii
- Lorca's production of *Blood Wedding* xxvi
- Other productions of *Blood Wedding* in Lorca's lifetime xxix
- Critical approaches to *Blood Wedding* xxxi
- Production history
  - Spanish productions xxxvi
  - US productions xxxviii
  - British productions xlii
- Translating Lorca xlviii

Further Reading liii

BLOOD WEDDING
- Act One 3
- Act Two 22
- Act Three 44

Notes 64

Questions for Further Study 98

Federico García Lorca: 1898–1936

1898 Born on 5 June in the village of Fuente Vaqueros in the province of Granada, the eldest of the four children of Don Federico García Rodríguez, a wealthy farmer and landowner, and Doña Vicenta Lorca Romero, a former schoolteacher in the village.

1907 The family moves to the village of Asquerosa, later called Valderrubio, only three miles from Fuente Vaqueros, where Don Federico buys a large house.

1908–09 Attends a boarding school in the town of Almería, some seventy miles from Granada, but his stay there is cut short by illness.

1909 Don Federico moves the family to Granada, the city which was to play such an important part in Lorca's work. He attends a small private school, the College of the Sacred Heart of Jesus, which, despite its name, is free of clerical influence. He is much more interested in music, in particular in playing the piano, than in his academic studies.

1914–15 After failing the second part of his final secondary education examinations in 1914, he retakes it successfully in the following year and, at the instigation of his parents, enters the Faculties of Philosophy and Letters and of Law at the University of Granada. His university career proves to be less than remarkable, but he comes under the influence of two distinguished professors: Martín Domínguez Berrueta, Professor of the Theory of Literature and the Arts, and Fernando de los Ríos Urruti, Professor of Political and Comparative Law. His musical abilities continue to develop under the teaching of Don Antonio Segura. He joins the Arts Club in Granada and also begins to frequent the Café Alameda, a meeting-place for the intellectuals and artists of the town, as well as for foreign visitors such as H. G. Wells, Rudyard Kipling and Artur Rubinstein.

1916 Study trips in May and October, organised by Domínguez Berrueta, to various Spanish towns and cities.

1917 In the spring and summer two further study trips. Lorca begins to write poetry, prose and short plays. Much of the poetry is concerned with sexual love and reveals the conflict in his mind between sexual desire and Catholic sexual morality.

1918 With the financial assistance of his father, Lorca publishes *Impressions and Landscapes*, a book based on his earlier travels with Domínguez Berrueta.

1919 In Granada meets Gregorio Martínez Sierra, a Madrid theatre producer, who encourages him to write a play about an injured butterfly (*The Butterfly's Evil Spell*), and the great Spanish composer, Manuel de Falla, with whom he begins an influential friendship. Moves from Granada to Madrid, commencing a ten-year stay at the Residencia de Estudiantes, an educational institution based on the Oxbridge college system. Meets Luis Buñuel, the future film director, who had entered the Residencia in 1917.

1920 *The Butterfly's Evil Spell* premiered at the Teatro Eslava in Madrid on 22 March but closes after four performances. Audience hostility towards a play about cockroaches, a butterfly and a scorpion is accompanied by poor reviews.

1921 Publication in Madrid of Lorca's first volume of poetry, *Book of Poems*.

1922 Completes a play for puppets, *The Tragicomedy of Don Cristóbal and Señorita Rosita*. In February Lorca lectures on 'deep song' (flamenco song) at the Arts Club in Granada, and, with Manuel de Falla and Miguel Cerón, helps to organise the Festival of Deep Song, held on 13 and 14 of June in the Alhambra's Plaza de los Aljibes. In anticipation of these events, he had written in the previous year a series of poems inspired by 'deep song' which he hoped to publish in conjunction with the festival.

1923 Organises with Manuel de Falla a puppet show which includes Lorca's own puppet play, *The Girl who Waters the Basil Plant*, and which takes place on 6 January in the García Lorcas' large flat in Granada. In the same month Lorca completes his law degree. In the Residencia he embarks on his important friendship with Salvador Dalí.

1924 Works on a collection of poems, *Gypsy Ballads*, on his second full-length play, *Mariana Pineda*, and on another play strongly influenced by the puppet tradition, *The Shoemaker's Wonderful Wife*. At the Residencia he becomes friendly with Rafael Alberti, who would soon become one of Spain's leading poets.

1925 Stays with Salvador Dalí and his sister, Ana María, at the family homes in Cadaqués and Figueras. Reads *Mariana Pineda* to them. Visits and is much impressed by Barcelona. Back in Granada writes several short plays, of which *Buster Keaton's Spin* and *The Maiden, the Sailor and the Student* survive.

1926 Completes *The Love of Don Perlimplín for Belisa in his Garden*. In Granada he delivers an important lecture, 'The Poetic Image in Don Luis de Góngora', on the great seventeenth-century Spanish poet. Publishes *Ode to Salvador Dalí*.

1927 Premiere of *Mariana Pineda*, to great acclaim, on 24 June at the Teatro Goya in Barcelona. Lorca exhibits twenty-four of his drawings at the Galerías Dalmau in the same city. Publishes *Songs*, his second volume of poems. *Mariana Pineda* opens at the Teatro Fontalba in Madrid on 12 October and is enthusiastically received.

1928 Edits the first issue of the literary magazine, *Cockerel*. He becomes involved with a young sculptor, Emilio Aladrén, to whom he is passionately attracted. At the end of July *Gypsy Ballads* is published to great critical acclaim, but is criticised by Dalí and Buñuel for being too traditional and not sufficiently avant-garde. During the summer Lorca feels depressed. In the autumn he delivers two lectures to the Athenaeum Club in Granada, 'Imagination, Inspiration and Escape in Poetry', and 'Sketch of the New Painting'.

1929 The Madrid premiere of *The Love of Don Perlimplín for Belisa in his Garden* is banned by the authorities. On 29 April *Mariana Pineda* opens triumphantly at the Teatro Cervantes in Granada. Emilio Aladrén begins to be involved romantically with the English girl he would marry two years later. This, together with anxieties about his deteriorating relationship with Dalí and about his work and his growing fame, exacerbates his depression. His family decide to send him to New York in the company of Fernando de los Ríos, where, after visiting Paris, London, Lucton School near Ludlow, Oxford, and Southampton, he arrives on 19 June. Enrols as a student of English at Columbia University, visits Harlem, then spends the summer in Vermont before returning to New York. Witnesses the Wall Street Crash. Works on *Poet in New York* and writes *Trip to the Moon*, a screenplay for the silent cinema, inspired in part by a visit to Coney Island but expressing too his own sexual anxieties.

1930 Leaves New York for Cuba, arriving in Havana on 7 March. Works on *The Public* and on *Ode to Walt Whitman*. Returns to Spain at the end of June. *The Shoemaker's Wonderful Wife* premiered in Madrid at the Teatro Español on 24 December.

1931 Publication of *Poem of Deep Song*. Completes *When Five Years Pass*. Appointed by the new left-wing Republican government as the artistic director of the Teatro Universitario, a touring theatre group which came to be known as 'La Barraca'. For the next four years the company would perform the great Spanish plays of the sixteenth and seventeenth centuries in the towns and villages of rural Spain as part of the government's broad-based educational programme.

1932 Lorca works on *Blood Wedding*. Reads *Poet in New York* in Barcelona.

1933 Premiere of *Blood Wedding* on 8 March at the Teatro Beatriz in Madrid, acclaimed by all the critics. *The Love of Don Perlimplín for Belisa in his Garden* premiered at the Teatro Español in Madrid on 5 April. Lorca works on *Yerma* and in October travels to Argentina where he both lectured and attended productions of his own plays: *Blood Wedding* and *The Shoemaker's Wonderful Wife*, both triumphantly received in Buenos Aires.

1934 *Mariana Pineda* opens in Buenos Aires on 12 January but receives only lukewarm reviews. Lorca's adaptation of Lope de Vega's *The Foolish Lady* is specially performed for an audience of actors. He arrives in Spain once again on 11 April and recommences work with 'La Barraca'. The bullfighter Ignacio Sánchez Mejías, a close friend of Lorca, receives fatal wounds in the bullring in Manzanares on 11 August. Shortly afterwards Lorca begins writing *Lament for Ignacio Sánchez Mejías* and also works on *Doña Rosita the Spinster*. On 29 December *Yerma* opens at the Teatro Español in Madrid. Despite an attempt by the Right to disrupt the performance, the play is received with great enthusiasm by both audience and critics.

1935 *The Shoemaker's Wonderful Wife* opens at the Madrid Coliseum on 18 March. Publication of *Lament for Ignacio Sánchez Mejías. The Puppet Show of Don Cristóbal* performed in the Paseo de Recoletos during the Madrid Book Fair. Lorca's version of *The Foolish Lady* is performed in both Madrid and Barcelona. *Yerma* opens in Barcelona on 17 September. Lorca works on *Sonnets of Dark Love* and on *Play Without a Title. Blood Wedding* opens in Barcelona on 22 November at the Principal Palace Theatre, to be followed by the triumphant premiere, on 12 December, of *Doña Rosita the Spinster*.

1936 Increasing political trouble in Spain. The Right and Centre parties defeated by the left-wing Popular Front in the February General Election. In the following months Lorca's socialist sympathies are increasingly in evidence. Publishes *Six Galician Poems* and *First Songs*. Works on *The Dreams of My Cousin Aurelia, Blood Has No Voice* (now lost), and *Play Without a Title*. Rehearsals of *When Five Years Pass* for a production at the Anfistora Club. *The House of Bernarda Alba* is completed on 19 June and in the following week reads the play to groups of his friends. Political unrest continues and Lorca leaves Madrid for Granada on 13 July. Five days later Franco initiates a military uprising against the Madrid government. The military in Granada rise on 20 July. Lorca, fearing the worst, takes refuge in the house of a fellow poet and friend, Luis Rosales. He is taken away from there on 16 August and detained in the Civil Government building. In the early hours of 18 August he is driven by Francoist thugs to a building outside the village of Viznar, north-east of Granada. From there he is taken by lorry, together with three other men, and shot in the olive groves which cover the slopes above the road to the village of Alfacar. In 1940 the authorities in Granada attempted to conceal the assassination by declaring that Lorca had died 'in the month of August 1936 from war wounds'.

Plot

Before the action of the play begins, the Mother has experienced the death of both her husband, after only three years of marriage, and later her elder son in a knife-fight with members of the Félix family, still imprisoned for their crimes. The feud between the two families, probably over land, is long-standing and makes her fear for the safety of her one remaining son, the Bridegroom, who now looks after the fields and vineyards once cultivated by the two dead men. The Bridegroom has, for the past three years, been courting the Bride, a young woman of twenty-two who lives with her widowed father, also a farmer, in 'the dry lands', four hours' drive by cart from the Mother's farm. Before meeting the Bridegroom, the Bride had been involved, at the age of fifteen, with Leonardo Félix, but their relationship had come to an end on account of his poor financial prospects and pressure exerted on her by the Father to seek a better marriage. Two years later Leonardo married the Bride's cousin and they now have a small child and another on the way.

Act One

Scene One

The curtain rises as the Bridegroom prepares to go off to work in the vineyard. Intending to eat grapes rather than the food which the Mother has prepared for him, he asks her for a knife with which to cut them, a request which immediately triggers in her both grief for her dead husband and son, rage at those responsible for their death, and fear for the Bridegroom's safety. The Bridegroom, accustomed to but also weary of the Mother's outbursts, attempts to distract her by introducing the subject of his desire to marry. Although she does not know the girl in question, she agrees to accompany her son to the girl's home the following Sunday and formally ask for her hand in marriage. Promising the Mother that he will make her happy with grandchildren, the Bridegroom leaves.

When a Neighbour comes to visit her, the Mother, anxious about her son's proposed marriage, takes the opportunity to question her about his bride-to-be. The Neighbour reveals, firstly, that the Bride's mother, to whom the Bride bears a strong physical resemblance, did not love her husband, and, secondly, that, when she was fifteen, the Bride's boy-friend was Leonardo Félix. The mere mention of the Félix family – the murderers of her husband and her son – fills the Mother with loathing and fear. As the Neighbour leaves, the Mother crosses herself in the hope of warding off the catastrophe she most fears.

Scene Two
The house of Leonardo Félix. The Wife is knitting while her mother cradles the child in her arms. They both sing a lullaby in an attempt to get the child to sleep – a dark lullaby about a horse whose hooves are bleeding and who will not drink from the stream. As the lullaby ends, Leonardo enters, returning from the blacksmith's where new shoes have been put on his horse. The Wife informs him that the neighbours have seen him recently on the far side of the plain in the dry lands and that she too has seen the horse half-dead from exhaustion. Leonardo's denial is almost immediately contradicted by the Mother-in-Law who declares that at this very moment the horse is down below in a state of virtual collapse. The Wife reveals to Leonardo that her cousin, the Bride, is to be married within the month and that they will probably be invited to the wedding. Leonardo reacts angrily both to the Mother-in-Law's reference to the fact that he was once the Bride's boy-friend and to the Girl who now enters and describes the presents bought for the Bride by the Bridegroom and his mother. The Girl leaves in tears and Leonardo storms out. The Wife and the Mother-in-Law again sing the lullaby. Both women begin to weep.

Scene Three
The home of the Bride and the Father: a cave in the dry lands which has been transformed into an attractive dwelling. The Mother and the Bridegroom arrive in order to request formally the

hand of the Bride in marriage. They have travelled for four hours in order to get there. The Father welcomes them, he and the Mother discuss their respective farms, as well as the attributes of the young couple, and the wedding-ceremony is arranged for the following week. The Bride enters but does not appear to be as happy as one might expect. The Father bids farewell to the Mother and the Bridegroom. Alone with the Servant, the Bride is downcast and disinterested in seeing her fiancé's presents. When the Servant reveals that during the night she saw Leonardo at the Bride's window, the Bride at first denies it, but then admits that he was there.

Act Two

Scene One
Four days later, the day of the wedding. It is early morning, intensely hot. Outside the cave, because it is cooler, the Servant is helping the Bride to get dressed for the ceremony. The Bride is uneasy and impatient with the Servant and throws the orange-blossom to the floor. The Servant begins to sing a wedding-song and the Bride seems more content. Leonardo is the first of the guests to arrive. He bitterly reminds the Bride of their former relationship and suggests that she abandoned him only because he was poor. Nothing, however, can eradicate their passion for each other, for when the roots of things go deep, no one can pull them up. The Bride's reaction confirms the truth of his words but, as the wedding guests are heard approaching, singing the song heard earlier, Leonardo is forced to leave.

The guests enter as dawn breaks. Their song of love and marriage envelops the Bride when she appears in her black wedding-dress and the Bridegroom when he arrives. In this atmosphere of celebration the Mother's fears return as she sees Leonardo. The Bride vows her love and loyalty to the Bridegroom, and the wedding party sets out for the church as the sun rises. Leonardo and his wife are the last to leave. The Wife voices her fear of being thrown aside even though she is expecting a second child, for such was her mother's fate. She begins to weep as the sound of the wedding-song rises triumphantly.

Scene Two
The Servant sets out trays of drinks for the guests returning from the wedding-ceremony. As she works, she sings a song in anticipation of the wedding-night. The Mother and the Father return from the church, but learn from the Servant that Leonardo and his wife have preceded them. His mere presence fills the Mother with foreboding, but she is encouraged by the Father to put the past behind her and look forward to a new future with grandchildren. The guests enter happily, surrounding the bridal couple. There is much revelry but within the general celebration there are discordant notes. The Bride is on edge. She reacts angrily to two young girls who ask her about her wedding-pins, and is strangely frightened when the Bridegroom embraces her from behind. Claiming that her head hurts, she goes to lie down, refusing to let her husband go with her. Soon afterwards the Father enters, revealing that he cannot find her, and a few moments later Leonardo's wife rushes in with the news that he and the Bride have run away. The Mother, telling the Father that his daughter is no better than his wife, urges the Bridegroom to pursue the lovers and cleanse the family name in blood.

Act Three

Scene One
Deep in a forest at night three Woodcutters appear to the accompaniment of two violins. They comment, like the Chorus in a Greek tragedy, on the runaway lovers, observing that they cannot deny their natural attraction to each other but that this will finally prove fatal. When they depart, imploring the rising moon to leave for the lovers a patch of shadow, the Moon enters in the form of a young white-faced woodcutter who, to alleviate his coldness, longs for the warmth of fresh blood. He leaves and is succeeded on stage by an old Beggar-Woman, who speaks ominously of deaths to come and who is immediately joined in her enterprise by a gloating and conspiratorial Moon. The Bridegroom enters in pursuit of the fleeing lovers and is directed by the Beggar-Woman to where they are hiding. After the Woodcutters have appeared once more, imploring that the lovers be spared, the Bride and Leonardo enter,

and in a series of powerful exchanges, express their deeply conflicting emotions: guilt and remorse on the one hand, the inescapability of their mutual passion on the other. They leave as they hear the sound of someone approaching. The Moon enters, filling the stage with a strong blue light. Two screams are heard. The Beggar-Woman appears and, with her back to the audience, opens her cloak like the wings of a great bird.

Scene Two

In a white room which has no sense of perspective and the simplicity of a church, two girls dressed in blue are winding a skein of red wool. Joined by a third girl, they seem like the three Fates and in their song not only announce that no one has returned from the wedding but that two men are dead 'on the silent shore'. The Mother-in-Law and Leonardo's wife enter, the former advising the Wife to accept the lonely and bitter life of a widow. When they leave, the Beggar-Woman appears, announcing triumphantly that the Bridegroom and Leonardo are dead and that their bodies are being brought on the shoulders of other young men. The girls leave and the Mother enters, accompanied by a neighbour. She speaks of her terrible grief but also of the consolation which lies in the fact that she need fear no more. When the Bride arrives, the Mother strikes her and the Bride attempts to explain to her that her passion for Leonardo was something she could not resist or control. The Mother treats her with indifference and, as she begins a final lament, sends the Bride to stand by the door. The Wife appears, and she and the Mother intone the lament for Leonardo and the Bridegroom. As the dead men are brought home and the neighbours kneel and weep, the words of the lamentation focus on the deaths which were decreed at a certain time on a certain day.

Commentary

Lorca and the theatre of his time

Lorca's dozen or so full-length plays, written during a relatively short period of sixteen years, reveal a great variety of influences, both Spanish and foreign. As far as European theatre in the first quarter of the twentieth century was concerned, there was amongst dramatists and practitioners who wished to see the theatre flourish and progress a clear reaction against the Naturalist movement of the nineteenth century. This, on balance, was a scientific approach which emphasised heredity and environment as the key 'determining' factors in the lives of human beings, and which, in terms of the theatre, led dramatists to attempt to recreate in their plays the here and now of everyday reality, in which both individuals and groups of people are shown to be influenced less by their own desires and aspirations than by those external pressures described above. In addition, and precisely because it emphasised the similarities rather than the differences between people, Naturalism in the theatre created a social levelling in terms of the classes presented on stage, and, as well as that, blurred both the distinctions between the 'high' and the 'low', the 'serious' and the 'comic', and those individual moments in a play which are 'dramatic' or 'undramatic'. The influence of Naturalism can be seen quite clearly in the plays of Anton Chekhov (1860–1904) and Henrik Ibsen (1828–1906), though both dramatists were, of course, responsive to other movements in the theatre.

Directly opposed to Naturalism, with its emphasis on the material world, was Symbolism, which was concerned with the transcendental, the greater reality which lies beyond the mundane world in which we live, and which had been anticipated in the nineteenth century in the theory and practice of such men as Richard Wagner. In his music drama Wagner had attempted to evoke through archetypal characters and by means of a theatrical technique which combined music, poetry, acting and stage design those eternal truths which lie beyond the visible world. As far as twentieth-century theatre is concerned, it was the Belgian dramatist Maurice Maeterlinck (1862–1949) who led the way. In *The Blue Bird*, written in 1905, two children, Tyltyl and Mytyl, embark on a quest to find the Blue Bird which will cure the sick child of a neighbour, are guarded by Light but obstructed by Night, and the Blue Bird escapes. The characters are clearly not so much individuals set in a particular time and space, as would have been the case in Naturalist drama, but archetypal beings who embody the very essence of human aspiration, struggle and ultimate failure, the symbolic nature of the characters and the stage action underpinned by stage design and movement which is highly stylised. In European theatre as a whole the same movement away from Naturalism was to be found in the theory and practice of such significant stage designers and directors as Adolph Appia, Edward Gordon Craig and Max Reinhardt, all of whom favoured symbolical representation and a close integration of the different elements of performance in order to stir the imagination of an audience.

The early years of the twentieth century were also marked by the development of other significant movements in the Arts, such as Cubism, Futurism, Dadaism, Expressionism, and later on, in the 1920s, Surrealism. In their different ways they are movements which represent both a rejection of hitherto accepted values and ideals, and an attempt to find new ways of looking at the world. Expressionism, dating from about 1910, was given an added impulse by the terrible atrocities of the 1914–18 War and was often concerned, therefore, with positive values such as the creation of an equal and just society and the rejection of the machine age in favour of a more simple society. In order to communicate its message Expressionist theatre, in the hands of dramatists such as Ernst Toller and Georg Kaiser, employed exaggeration and distortion in both characterisation, language and staging.

Surrealism, associated in particular with the Paris Surrealists of the 1920s but evident before that, was concerned in part with the unconscious mind, with the inner rather than the outer man, with the illogical and the irrational, and with the expression of feelings and emotions uncontrolled by reason. In the theatre in France, Guillaume Apollinaire and Jean Cocteau, in plays such as *The*

Breasts of Tiresias and *Parade*, both performed in 1917, set out to undermine the Naturalist tradition in order to suggest both the importance of the unconscious mind and the truth that lies beneath the appearance of things. In consequence, the technique of the plays lies at the very opposite extreme to Naturalism, employing all manner of exaggeration and distortion to evoke a world in which logic plays no part.

In Spain itself Naturalism had its equivalent in writers such as Benito Pérez Galdós (1843–1920), who, apart from being Spain's greatest novelist of the nineteenth century, also wrote twenty-two plays, and Jacinto Benavente (1866–1954), who dominated the Spanish theatrical scene for so many years. Both Galdós and Benavente reacted against the inflated neo-Romantic style which had characterised the theatre in the latter part of the nineteenth century, and both were concerned in their own plays with a greater realism in relation to characters, background and language. This said, the theatre of Benavente did not change or evolve very much during his long career. Having discovered a successful formula, he largely settled for it, and in his hands, as well as in the hands of a number of other successful and popular dramatists, Spanish theatre remained for many years rather stagnant and undemanding.

Of the dramatists who, influenced by cultural trends outside Spain, attempted to advance the cause of Spanish theatre through bold experiment, the most important figure before Lorca was undoubtedly Ramón del Valle-Inclán (1866–1936). His early work, in particular *The Savage Plays*, reveals the clear influence of European Symbolism, for it is concerned, in its portrayal of the history of Don Juan Manuel Montenegro and his family, with the evocation of timeless and universal issues, above all good and evil and the redemption of Man through suffering. Valle-Inclán's technique, moreover, is highly reminiscent in its synthesis of stage settings, costumes, movement, lighting and dialogue of the ideas on theatre of Symbolist stage designers and producers such as Adolphe Appia and Edward Gordon Craig.

By 1920, and partly in response to the horrors of the First World War, Valle-Inclán's Symbolist phase had given way to his theory and practice of the grotesque, *esperpentismo*, an approach to dramatic writing which is defined in *Bohemian Lights*, written in 1920, which owes something to Expressionism, as well as to the puppet tradition, and which Valle-Inclán believed more appropriate to the expression of the absurd and grotesque nature of Spanish life as he saw it. Other significant writers of the time who turned their back on Naturalism were Miguel de Unamuno (1864–1936), whose stark, unadorned plays often exteriorise emotional and intellectual conflicts, and Jacinto Grau (1877–1958), whose work after 1918 expresses the preoccupations of that time in a style which closely integrates the different elements of stage performance.

As far as Spain is concerned, mention must be made too of the important centuries-old tradition of puppet-theatre and farce. Cervantes, for example, had introduced a puppet show, *Master Peter's Puppet Show*, into the second part of *Don Quixote*, published in 1615, while the same year also saw the appearance of a collection of eight short plays, *Interludes*, which in their presentation of ingenious situations and boldly comic characters were models of their kind. Valle-Inclán in his grotesque plays, Jacinto Grau in *Mr Pygmalion*, written in 1921, and Carlos Arniches (1866–1943) in his *grotesque farces*, continued that tradition in the first two decades or so of the twentieth century.

Lorca's first play, *The Butterfly's Evil Spell*, reveals the very clear influence of Symbolism, as well as, in all probability, the direct influence of Maeterlinck's *The Blue Bird*. Through the story of Curianito, the young cockroach who falls in love with the Butterfly but is rejected by her, Lorca explores the themes of love, frustration and death which are so central to his own existence. This, moreover, is enhanced by Lorca's highly stylised presentation of the characters and events which transforms the particularity of the on-stage action into a visual metaphor with which we can all identify. There are strong elements of Symbolism too in Lorca's second play, *Mariana Pineda*, despite the fact that the subject is historical and, to that extent, more 'realistic'. Once more the themes are the characteristic Lorca themes of passion and frustration, but, as well as this, the purity of Mariana herself is set against the evil of Pedrosa, the Chief of Police, while the conflict between them, itself universal in its implications, is set within an essentially poetic and symbolic frame created by the white of walls and costume, the black of Pedrosa's clothes, and the approach of night. The concerns of Symbolism, including concepts of staging which are strictly anti-naturalistic, are to be found throughout Lorca's theatre.

At the same time, his interest in puppet-theatre was evident from an early stage. In 1922, two years after the disastrous opening of *The Butterfly's Evil Spell*, he completed a play for puppets, *The Tragicomedy of Don Cristóbal and Señorita Rosita*, and in the following year organised a puppet show in Granada with Manuel de Falla. It was an aspect of his work which was, in conjunction with farce, to become more important in the years ahead, for between 1924 and 1935 *The Shoemaker's Wonderful Wife, The Love of Don Perlimplín for Belisa in his Garden*, and *The Puppet Play of Don Cristóbal* were all written and performed.

Lorca's interest in this tradition and his championing of it in his own work is easily explained, for, like Symbolism, puppet-theatre and farce are anti-naturalistic, characterised by a simplicity and a boldness which allowed Lorca that freedom of expression, that spontaneity and vitality which he believed to be the essential ingredients of a living theatre. So, in the prologue to *The Puppet Play of Don Cristóbal* he refers to 'the delicious and hard language of the puppets', and later the director of the play itself wishes to 'fill the theatre with fresh wheat', a clear pointer to the stale Naturalism of much contemporary Spanish theatre. Although the characters of *The Shoemaker's Wonderful Wife* are played by actors, the technique is very much that of the puppet-play as they engage in vigorous physical and verbal action against settings which in their boldness echo the immediacy of the characters. They are features of Lorca's theatrical style which, in varying degrees, are to be seen in all his plays.

Surrealism came into its own in Lorca's work in the theatre in two major plays, *The Public* and *When Five Years Pass*, completed in 1930 and 1931 respectively, though its influence is evident both before and after these particular plays. Lorca's friendships with Luis Buñuel and Salvador Dalí proved crucial in relation to the dramatist's familiarity with 'avant-garde' movements in European culture, as well as to his exposure to the theories of Sigmund Freud, much read at the Residencia de Estudiantes in the 1920s. There are clear surrealist elements in the short piece, *Buster Keaton's Spin*, written in 1925, but it was the emotional crisis of 1929 which led Lorca to express his true inner anguish in the two full-length and enormously ambitious plays mentioned above. In both *The Public*, his only overtly gay play, and *When Five Years Pass*, arguably his most accomplished and striking piece of theatre, Lorca's personal obsessions – love, frustration, passing time and death – are expressed through an action which is essentially dreamlike, in which the characters are seen to be echoes of or contrasts to each other and in which their unconscious fears frequently assume frightening external forms. Thus, at a crucial moment in Act One of *When Five Years Pass*, the on-stage characters of the Young Man, the Old Man, the Friend and the Second Friend are suddenly confronted by a nightmarish scene involving the Dead Child and the Dead Cat which exteriorises the deep-seated anxieties of all the onlookers. Greatly influenced by Surrealism, both plays also reveal in their strongly visual character and in their fluid movement the imprint of Symbolism, Expressionism, puppet-theatre and cinema. Once more Lorca reveals himself to be a constant experimenter in his search for freedom of expression, a fundamental aspect of his work which is also evident in his screenplay of 1929, *Trip to the Moon*.

These various influences come together as well, of course, in Lorca's great plays of the 1930s, including the so-called 'rural trilogy' of *Blood Wedding*, *Yerma*, and *The House of Bernarda Alba*. In one sense plays whose subjects, characters and settings are located in the Spanish countryside and suggest Naturalism rather than any kind of stylisation, the opposite is in fact true, despite the fact that *Blood Wedding* and *The House of Bernarda Alba* have their origins in real-life events. In the first place, the names which Lorca gives his characters have, for the most part, a generic and archetypal quality: in *Blood Wedding* the Mother, the Father, the Bridegroom, the Bride, the Wife, the Neighbour; in *Yerma* the Old Woman, the First Girl, the Second Girl. And even when there are real names they often have a symbolic resonance: in *Blood Wedding* the two halves of Leonardo's name suggest a 'burning lion'; and in *The House of Bernarda Alba*, the surname Alba has associations with 'dawn' and therefore 'brightness' and 'light', while the connections of Angustias with anguish and Martirio with martyrdom are evident enough. In addition, Lorca's constant linking of the characters of these plays to the soil, the trees, the heat, water, the seasons, in short to the world of Nature, creates a very strong sense of their universality. In the final acts of *Blood Wedding* and *Yerma*, moreover, the effect is enhanced and a sense of timelessness created by the appearance of non-human figures: in the former Moon and Death (the Beggar-Woman); in the latter the fertility figures of Male and Female. Lorca's use of poetry in both plays, and especially in *Blood Wedding*, also has the effect of universalising the particular through suggestive metaphor, while his suggestions for staging – stark, stylised settings, dramatic lighting effects, and bold movement, including dance – reveal an intention at the opposite extreme from Naturalism. And even if, in *The House of Bernarda Alba*, the poetry of the other two plays is pared away and there seems to be a greater realism, a closer examination suggests that Lorca's predilection is still for an overall stylisation. Indeed, in their different ways the three plays of the rural trilogy can be seen to combine elements of Symbolism, Expressionism, Surrealism – consider the forest scene of *Blood Wedding* – and the puppet tradition, all fused into an anti-naturalistic style of which he increasingly proved to be a master.

Staging of Lorca's plays in his lifetime

The production of Lorca's first play, *The Butterfly's Evil Spell*, which opened at the Teatro Eslava in Madrid on 22 March 1920, was an unmitigated disaster. The original intention of the theatre impresario, Gregorio Martínez Sierra, was that the play should be performed by puppets, which might well have been more effective, but in the end it was presented by actors, the role of the Butterfly performed by the leading ballet dancer, Encarnación López Júlvez, 'La Argentina'. The set and costumes were extremely colourful and the music used at particular points in the play was by Grieg. From the outset a section of the audience, clearly hostile to any kind of experimentation in the theatre, seemed determined to ruin the evening, and the reviews which appeared in the following morning's newspapers were not much more encouraging.

Although Lorca worked on a number of puppet-plays and farces between 1922 and 1927, his second production was *Mariana Pineda*, which he had completed in 1924, and which was premiered at the Teatro Goya in Barcelona on 24 June 1927, the eponymous heroine played by the famous actress Margarita Xirgu, who would become increasingly involved in Lorca's work, and the sets designed by Salvador Dalí. Although the play was performed only six times in Barcelona, for Margarita Xirgu's company ended their season there on 28 June, it was warmly received by the critics, as was the case when the production opened in the following autumn at the Teatro Fontalba in Madrid. Contemporary reviews of the Madrid production emphasise both the highly poetic nature of Lorca's treatment of the historical subject, so familiar to Spaniards, and the stylisation of the production in which sets and costumes played such an important part. M. Fernández-Almagro, the theatre critic of the newspaper, *La Voz*, spoke of the exquisite simplicity of Dalí's designs, a view echoed by E. Díez-Canedo in *El Sol*. In short, despite the fact that *Mariana Pineda* was a historical play and therefore open to a naturalistic treatment, Lorca's poetic approach to it, underlined by the production itself, points to the general thrust of his theatre as a whole.

It was again Margarita Xirgu who played the lead part in the premiere of *The Shoemaker's Wonderful Wife* at the Teatro Español in Madrid on 24 December 1930. Particularly interesting about this production was the fact that Lorca himself, dressed in a star-spangled cloak, read the prologue in which the Author appears on stage and informs the audience of the need for poetry and magic on the contemporary stage. In terms of its staging, the play evidently put into practice Lorca's intentions, for the sets and costumes, based on drawings by the dramatist himself, and influenced by Picasso's designs for Manuel de Falla's *Three Cornered Hat*, matched the character of the play in their bold, vibrant colours and combined perfectly with vigorous movement and language in order to recreate on the modern stage all the vitality of a long puppet-play tradition. Lorca's piece ran for some thirty performances and greatly strengthened his working relationship with Margarita Xirgu.

The spring of 1933 saw two triumphant premieres which increased Lorca's fame as a playwright: *Blood Wedding* at the Teatro Beatriz in Madrid on 8 March, and *The Love of Don Perlimplín for Belisa in his Garden* on 5 April at the Teatro Español, both directed by Lorca himself. The production of *Blood Wedding* will be discussed in more detail later. Suffice it to say that Lorca's own work was now being influenced greatly by his own experience as a director with the touring company, 'La Barraca', which provided him with an ever deepening knowledge of the practicalities of performance. The reviews of *The Love of Don Perlimplin* point to the colourful stylisation of the production, enhanced by the music of Scarlatti. At the end of May 1933 the Madrid production of *Blood Wedding* opened in Barcelona, and in July another production of the play was a great success in Buenos Aires before going on tour and returning to the city in October. It ran for several months, made Lorca a good deal of money and established his reputation in Argentina. In December, moreover, the same company opened with *The Shoemaker's Wonderful Wife*, which proved to be equally successful.

Lola Membrives, whose company produced both plays in Buenos Aires, was anxious to stage another play of Lorca's in early 1934, and, in the absence of a new work, decided to present *Mariana Pineda*, which opened on 12 January. In spite of the fact that the famous actress took the part of Mariana, this early play of Lorca's was compared unfavourably with *Blood Wedding* and the production was not a great success. In complete contrast, *Yerma*, the second play in his rural trilogy, was a complete triumph when it opened on 29 December at the Teatro Español in Madrid, with Margarita Xirgu in the title role. Initially, right-wing extremists, enraged by Lorca's homosexuality and left-wing sympathies, as well as by Margarita Xirgu's support for Manuel Azaña, a leading left-wing politician who had recently been imprisoned, attempted to disrupt the performance, but were then thrown out of the theatre. When the curtain fell, the reaction of the audience was rapturous, and Lorca himself was obliged to make numerous appearances on stage. Writing in *El Sol* the following day, M. Fernández-Almagro spoke of the dramatist's stark, classical treatment of his subject matter, of Margarita Xirgu's instinctive feeling for every nuance of emotion and gesture on the part of the protagonist, and of the way in which the stage-design by Manuel Fontanals enhanced and harmonised with the action at every stage. With regard to the latter, Enrique Díez-Canedo, writing in *La Voz*, referred to Fontanal's broad effects, lacking in fussy realistic details, which formed the background to the action. And, as for the play itself, he drew attention to the important point that no one should fall into the trap of regarding Lorca's writing as naturalistic. It is, above all, poetic, but its poetry is strong and vibrant, without sentimentality.

1935 saw a number of important productions of Lorca's plays in Spain. While *Yerma* continued at the Teatro Español, the company of Lola Membrives had returned from Buenos Aires and on 28 February opened at the Madrid Coliseum with her production of *Blood Wedding*. Less than a month later the company, giving two performances each evening as was the Spanish practice, gave *Blood Wedding* at the first performance and *The Shoemaker's Wonderful Wife* at the second. In the first quarter of 1935 Lorca therefore had three plays running in Madrid, an unheard of event in the theatre of that time. By the middle of the year he had also finished writing *Doña Rosita the Spinster*, which Margarita Xirgu proposed to include in her forthcoming season in Barcelona. The season of one month at the Teatro Barcelona opened on 10 September with a production of Lorca's adaptation of Lope de Vega's *The Foolish Lady*, followed a week later by *Yerma*, the success of which was as great as it had been in Madrid. On 5 November the company performed *Yerma* at the Teatro Principal in Valencia, the second production in a short season there, and then returned to Barcelona where Margarita Xirgu would present both *Blood Wedding* and *Doña Rosita the Spinster* at the Principal Palace Theatre. The former opened on 22 November to great acclaim, the sets designed by José Caballero and the music directed by Lorca who also accompanied on the piano the lullaby in the second scene of Act One. If anything, the premiere of *Doña Rosita the Spinster* on 12 December was an even greater success. In this play, set in Granada, and in which, over a period of twenty-five years, Rosita waits in vain for her fiancé to return and hope gradually gives way to a realisation of the hopelessness of her situation, Lorca had evoked both his own experience of love and the beautiful, magical, sad and introverted city in which he had spent so much of his life. Essentially different from *Blood Wedding* and *Yerma* in its subject matter, *Doña Rosita the Spinster* has something of the bitter-sweetness of Chekhov, a point not lost on the critics who praised it the following day. Writing in *La Vanguardia*, María Luz Rosales commented in particular on the way in which the play induced laughter and tears at the same time, and on how, through both prose and poetry, the mood of Granada through a quarter of a century is so delicately and evocatively created by the writer. In Barcelona Lorca's play was performed to packed houses, regular articles about him appeared in the newspapers, a special performance of the play was put on for the flower-sellers of the Ramblas, and at the end of the year there was a magnificent banquet at the Majestic Inglaterra Hotel, attended by Catalonia's artists and intellectuals. Lorca was indeed at the height of his fame.

In January 1936 Margarita Xirgu left Spain for Cuba, where, on 16 February she presented *Yerma* in Havana to enthusiastic audiences. On 18 April she opened her season in Mexico with the same play and subsequently presented *Doña Rosita the Spinster*, *The Shoemaker's Wonderful Wife* and *Blood Wedding*. In Spain itself there were to be no productions, although Lorca was at work, as always, on a variety of projects. The work which has been discussed above, as well as the plays he was now either writing or planning, provide abundant evidence of the extent to which he was always eager to experiment and seek new forms of theatrical expression. But what is even more surprising is the fact that such an innovative dramatist should also have triumphed in the commercial theatre of his day.

Lorca's production of *Blood Wedding*

The premiere of *Blood Wedding* at the Teatro Beatriz in Madrid on 8 March 1933 was a triumph for Lorca. During the rehearsal period, however, he had encountered numerous problems with his actors, some of which had severely tested his patience. In this context it has to be borne in mind that in this play Lorca had combined prose and poetry in a manner which was quite unusual in Spanish theatre, for until then the two were largely separate. The actors were therefore not accustomed to switching from one style to another in the same play, and many of them experienced great difficulty in speaking the lines as Lorca wanted them spoken. His brother, Francisco, who attended the rehearsals, has observed that the actor who played the Bridegroom presented an almost insurmountable obstacle, for his experience was entirely in light comedy, and he therefore found it extremely difficult to escape the strait-jacket of that tradition. Furthermore, the woodcutters of Act Three, Scene One, who in effect play the part of the chorus and whose lines have a strong rhythmic quality, were played by actors who were not only very average but who had probably never spoken verse in their entire acting careers. It was the only occasion when Francisco saw his brother lose his temper as a director.

Blood Wedding also posed problems of performance in the sense that it combined to a degree quite unusual in the Spanish theatre of the time all the different elements of stage performance: language, movement, costume, lighting and music. The actors were faced, therefore, not only with the problems posed by prose and poetry, but also with the difficulties created by the many occasions in the play which involve groups of people, both men and women, sometimes on different stage-levels, when the dialogue passes from one to another in an almost musical fashion. In this respect Lorca's brother mentions the Bride's departure for the church at the end of Act Two, Scene One, as being particularly difficult. In rehearsals Lorca insisted at this point of the play on 'mathematical precision and precise timing', as indeed he must have done in relation to many other complex moments in the text. In this respect he was putting into practice the knowledge which he had acquired over several years by directing the touring theatre company 'La Barraca', and he was always completely sure of the effect he wanted to achieve. The actors, it seems, were greatly impressed by his skill as a director.

The premiere at the Teatro Beatriz has been vividly described by Carlos Morla Lynch, a Chilean diplomat and a great friend of Lorca. In the audience were the best-known dramatists, poets and intellectuals of the day: Jacinto Benavente, the Alvarez Quintero brothers, Eduardo Marquina, Vicente Aleixandre, Luis Cernuda, Jorge Guillén, Pedro Salinas, and Miguel de Unamuno. Morla Lynch notes that by the end of Act One the audience had been completely won over, and such was their enthusiasm by the end of Act Two, Scene One, that Lorca was obliged to come on stage in order to receive their applause. When the final curtain fell, the ovation was instantaneous and Lorca took numerous curtain-calls along with the leading actress, Josefina Díaz de Artigas, who played the Bride, and the set and costume designers, Santiago Ontañón and Manuel Fontanals.

The account of Morla Lynch, taken in conjunction with the reviews of the premiere which appeared in the Madrid newspapers the following day, suggest quite clearly the kind of production which *Blood Wedding* was given at the Teatro Beatriz. In relation to the stage-design, for example, Morla Lynch noted that when the curtain rose on Act One, Scene One, it revealed a simple room in different tonalities of yellow; in Scene Two a room painted pink; for the final scene of Act Three a room painted white. In short, the set-design captured the stylisation which Lorca had in mind and which is suggested very clearly by the stage directions of the published text. The point was reinforced by the reviews of the following day. M. Fernández-Almagro, writing in *El Sol*, drew particular attention to the way in which backgrounds of pink and white, for example, harmonised with the mood of particular scenes. Morla Lynch was impressed too by the musical qualities of the play's language. He mentions the magical yet sinister effect of the lullaby in Act One, Scene Two, and, in total contrast, the songs of the wedding guests in Act Two, Scene One, which grew in intensity as the scene unfolded, a great hymn of joy which drew from the audience a tremendous ovation and obliged Lorca to appear on stage. M. Nuñez de Arenas, in *La Voz*, also drew attention to the extraordinary beauty of the language of the play, mentioning, in addition to the lullaby and the songs of the wedding guests, the choral nature of the woodcutters' lines and the speeches of the Mother. For Fernández-Almagro, furthermore, the characters on stage were not simply ordinary peasants in a particular time and place. They were, above all, the very embodiment of the tragic spirit of Andalusia from time immemorial; archetypal characters who voiced universal experiences and emotions which would touch men and women everywhere. As for individual performances, the theatre critic of *ABC* picked out for special praise Josefina Díaz de Artigas, Josefina Tapias, and Manuel Collado, who played the Bride, the Mother and the Bridegroom respectively. Given the problems Lorca had with Manuel Collado in rehearsal, they seem to have been largely overcome by the first night. Indeed, all the critics seem to have been impressed by the actors – tribute in part to Lorca's skill as a director – the only dissenting voice belonging to Nuñez de Arenas who, in *La Voz*, criticised Josefina Díaz de Artigas for a particular hand movement which he found mannered and unconvincing. What emerges above all from the various accounts of this premiere, however, is the emphasis which Lorca and the other members of his team placed on stylisation in every aspect of the performance and which ran very much against the current of the kind of productions which dominated the commercial theatre in Madrid at that time.

Other productions of *Blood Wedding* in Lorca's lifetime

After the triumph of *Blood Wedding* at the Teatro Beatriz, the production transferred with equal success to Barcelona, where it opened at the Poliorama Theatre on 31 May. Subsequently, its reputation in Lorca's lifetime was consolidated by two actresses who ran their own companies: Lola Membrives and Margarita Xirgu. Lola Membrives had opened her season at the Maipo Theatre in Buenos Aires on 22 May 1933, and presented a number of plays by contemporary Spanish dramatists, none of which had enthused the theatre-going public of the city. Before staging *Blood Wedding*, she read the play to a group of critics who reacted to it with enthusiasm, and therefore decided to go ahead immediately with her production. It opened on 29 July with Lola Membrives herself playing the Mother and was an instant success, acclaimed by the public and the critics alike. The theatre critic of *La Nación* observed that *Blood Wedding* was by far the best play in Lola Membrives's season, as well as the most impressive play for many years of those which had come from Spain to Buenos Aires. It ran in fact for twenty consecutive performances, until 7 August, when the company embarked on a tour of the provinces before returning to Buenos Aires, where the play's second run in 1933 opened at the Teatro Avenida on 25 October. By this time Lorca himself had arrived in Buenos Aires and, when he appeared on stage to address the audience before the curtain went up, he was greeted with a standing ovation. Once more the evening was a triumph. On a larger stage the play proved even more effective than it had been at the Maipo Theatre, the audience applauded the conclusion of each scene with enormous enthusiasm, and, at the end, provided a second standing ovation for Lorca.

Subsequently, the production ran for several months, earning him a great deal of money and consolidating his reputation in Argentina. In 1934 Lola Membrives staged *Blood Wedding* once more at the Teatro Avenida where it opened on 1 March. By the time she and her company returned to Spain in the autumn, she had performed *Blood Wedding* 150 times. In Spain itself her Buenos Aires production opened on 28 February 1935 at the Madrid Coliseum to considerable critical acclaim.

Margarita Xirgu's association with Lorca had commenced in 1926, when he had given her a copy of *Mariana Pineda*. In the following year she staged the play with considerable success in Barcelona and followed it up with an equally successful run in Madrid in the autumn. At the end of 1930 she took the lead part in another successful production of *The Shoemaker's Wonderful Wife* at the Teatro Español in Madrid, and in December 1934 in the same theatre played the part of Yerma in the triumphant premiere of the play of the same name. Lorca's association with the great Catalan actress was therefore longer and closer than with any other actress of that time, and it is, in a way, surprising that she was not involved in the premiere of *Blood Wedding*. She finally staged the play at the Principal Palace Theatre in Barcelona, where it opened on 22 November 1935.

This third major production of the play in the space of three years was not directed by Lorca himself but by Cipriano Rivas Cherif, the artistic adviser to Margarita Xirgu and himself a leading figure in the Spanish theatre of the day. Lorca, however, acted as musical director, wrote some of the music, and in the production accompanied on the piano the lullaby of Act One, Scene Two, as well as the wedding-songs. As far as the stage design was concerned, Lorca had written to the stage designer, José Caballero, prior to the opening, suggesting that for the forest scene of Act Three the curtain should have on it a great white horse against a background of mountains on a moonlit night. Two days later he had decided against using it, but his suggestion points very clearly to the stylisation of the production as a whole.

The production delighted Lorca, the audience and the critics. María Luz Morales, writing in *La Vanguardia*, drew attention to the quality which Rivas Cherif and Lorca had brought to the staging, as well as to the moving interpretation by Margarita

Xirgu of the role of the Mother. The actress had succeeded, above all, in suggesting the character's inner anguish, as much by what she did not say as by what she said, and in the part realised one of her greatest interpretations. As for the dramatist, Domènec Guansé, writing in *La Publicitat*, noted that Lorca seemed to him 'a poet who made theatre', and added that 'by virtue of his sincerity, his emotion, his poetic inspiration, his desire to seek the essential truth of things, his determination to avoid the flashy and banal, García Lorca is, in our theatre, the most authoritative interpreter of the Andalusian soul'. Two months later, in January 1936 Margarita Xirgu left Spain for Latin America and included *Blood Wedding* in her season in Mexico, which began on 18 April. If, as was her wish, Lorca had joined her there, he would have avoided the terrible fate that overtook him just a few months later.

Critical approaches to *Blood Wedding*

Although there are no particular schools of thought in Lorca studies, as is often the case in English literary criticism, it is true to say that individual critics have adopted particular approaches which distinguish their work. One of these is the view that in the plays and poetry which have an Andalusian background, Lorca attempted to express not the here-and-now of this vast and fascinating region but its ancient, often tragic, and eternal spirit. In a lecture on Andalusian 'deep song' or flamenco, given in 1922, Lorca himself observed that flamenco song is 'the cry of dead generations, the piercing elegy of centuries now gone', and that it 'comes from distance races, crossing the cemetery of the years and the trailing foliage of winds now withered. It comes from the first sob and the first kiss'. Similarly, when commenting on his volume of poetry, *Gypsy Ballads*, published in 1928 and in which the gypsies of Andalusia are the focal point, Lorca suggested that the poems were 'a myth invented by me... I am trying to harmonise that which is mythical in the gypsy with that which is everyday and commonplace.' In short, he was himself perfectly aware of the broader resonances of his work.

The review by Fernández-Almagro of the Madrid premiere of *Blood Wedding* points in the same direction: 'What impressed me most in *Blood Wedding* is precisely that: the spirit which drives the entire piece, a breath which comes from a great distance and a great depth. The spirit of a primitive people ... which does not refer to the Andalusians of the East or West, the mountains or the coast, but to the Andalusians in their deepest psychological and historical projection. To those who were and continue to be: Arabs, Greeks, Romans, children of who knows which classical myths: the sun and the moon.' It is a view which has been taken up in particular by Allen Josephs and Juan Caballero in their collaborative work on Lorca.

Josephs and Caballero argue that, for a variety of reasons, Andalusia was in Lorca's time very firmly rooted in the past and that its links with the ancient classical world remained strong. This was, moreover, something of which Lorca was always aware, in particular of powerful links between Ancient Greece and Andalusia, which, for him, manifested themselves, amongst other things, in the tragic spirit of the latter. As far as theatre was concerned, therefore, Lorca was the declared enemy of the bourgeois theatre of his day with its emphasis on good taste and restraint and an ardent advocate of a theatre which, in the manner of Aeschylus, Sophocles and Euripides, was uncompromising in its exposure of terrible truths and powerful passions. Greek tragedy has at its very heart human characters who are overwhelmed by forces which are greater than themselves and which they can neither control nor understand. It was a world which, for Lorca, still existed in rural Andalusia with its deep-rooted beliefs in the forces of the supernatural and the irrational and the powerlessness of the individual in relation to them. For these reasons, Josephs and Caballero suggest, he is one of the few dramatists of the twentieth century who have had no problems in writing tragedy.

In *Blood Wedding* Josephs and Caballero draw attention to the prominence of the knife, which in the ancient religions was the instrument of sacrifice: the Bridegroom and Leonardo are the sacrificial victims, acknowledged as such by the grieving women in the closing scene. Their sacrificial death is presided over by a divinity – not the god-bull Dionysius here, but the Moon which in Act Three takes on the character of ancient myth, embodying all the mystery and power of the ancient, pre-Christian world. To this extent the world depicted by Lorca in *Blood Wedding* is one which is entirely removed from modern, mechanised society. Rather it is a world ruled by forces over which, as in the ancient world, human beings have no control. In terms of stage performance, Lorca intended the play to have a strong element of music and dance which, in particular in the case of the chorus, would evoke the emotions of Greek tragedy and finally awaken in the audience both a recognition and acceptance of those elemental forces which at any moment may sweep human beings to their doom.

The Spanish critic Gustavo Correa situates the characters and the action of *Blood Wedding* very firmly within the processes and cycles of the natural world (*La poesía mítica de Federico García Lorca*, Editorial Gredos, 1975, pp. 82–116). In this respect the notion of the continuity of family through the marriage of the Bride and the Bridegroom is linked to the continuity of Nature itself, and the identification between the human characters of the play and the world in which they live is established by a close-knit pattern of images – earth, crops, trees, rivers, climate, animals – which constantly relate human and natural forms. The Mother is therefore associated with the earth, Leonardo with a fast-flowing river, the passive Bridegroom with a tiny drop of water. The forces which are at work in the world of Nature, and which may be both positive and negative, have their counterparts, moreover, in the lives of men and women. The instincts which determine the actions and the lives of animals exist too in human beings and may, depending on the circumstances, be either positive or negative. When the sexual instincts of a man and a woman draw them to each other in an arrangement which accords with the requirements of a particular society, their union will have positive consequences. If, on the other hand, their instincts draw them to each other in circumstances of which society does not approve, their union will have negative results. But what cannot in the end be denied are the demands of instinct and inclination, as powerful and as irresistible in the world of men and animals as in the world of Nature. In *Blood Wedding* the Bride and Leonardo exemplify this fact, their attraction to each other as irreversible as the coming of day and night or the movements of the seasons themselves. Instinct is thus the equivalent of fate, which in their case sweeps them to disaster but which, in different circumstances, might equally have brought about a different end.

It is, perhaps, in relation to the question and the nature of tragedy in Lorca's theatre that critical opinions have proved to be most divided. One approach, represented by C. L. Halliburton, is that in *Blood Wedding* Lorca put into practice the traditional Aristotelian/Renaissance definition of tragedy ('García Lorca, the Tragedian: An Aristotelian Analysis of *Bodas de sangre*'), whereby the play's protagonist has admirable qualities but is also flawed. In the course of the action that flaw is worked upon by circumstances or fate, which in turn brings about the downfall and even the death of the character in question and awakens in the spectator of the action a response which balances admiration for the character's qualities with a feeling of pity and even of fear for the fate which befalls him or her: the catharsis or purging of emotion. Although there is no single protagonist in *Blood Wedding*, the Mother, the Bridegroom and the Bride all have good qualities. The Bride, for example, wishes to obey and please her father, as well as to be loyal to her husband, while the Mother wishes only for her son's future happiness. But in both cases good intentions are swept aside by a flaw – the Bride's ineradicable passion for Leonardo, the Mother's ingrained hatred of Leonardo's family – which, worked upon by fate, brings about the deaths of the Bridegroom and Leonardo, the disgrace and downfall of the Bride, and the Mother's desperate anguish: events which awaken in the audience intense feelings of both admiration and pity.

The view outlined by Halliburton and others has been forcibly rejected by D. L. Shaw, who argues that the Aristotelian/Renaissance concept of tragedy rests, by definition, on a belief in a universe which is ultimately ordered ('Lorca's Late Plays and the Idea of Tragedy', in *Essays on Hispanic Themes in Honour of Edward C. Riley*, University of Edinburgh, 1972, pp. 200–8). Thus, the evil which unleashes itself in *Macbeth* is, though terrible, only temporary, and, with the death of Macbeth himself, gives way to order with the arrival of Malcolm and the hope of better things to come. Furthermore, the very existence of a flaw in a character suggests the existence of a good from which the character in question has departed. For Shaw the tragedies of Lorca stand at the opposite extreme, for he considers the notion of an ordered universe or a final consolation to be entirely absent from them. *Blood Wedding* is the perfect example of a world in which human beings are destroyed by passions which they can do nothing to control, and the ending of the play is one which, far from providing any kind of solace, leaves the audience in a condition of lost hope. Lorca is, indeed, a dramatist who captures the essential spirit of the modern world from which a sense of the order of things is largely absent.

My own view ('The Way Things Are: Towards a Definition of Lorcan Tragedy', in *Anales de la Literatura Española Contemporánea*, 1996, pp. 271–90) is that Lorca's concept of tragedy has its origins in his sexuality, which must have led him not only to question the way things are but to believe that he was somehow fated. This, combined with the emphasis placed on fate and destiny in the culture of Andalusia, helped to shape in him a keen awareness of the often tragic nature of human life and of the constant clash within it of aspiration on the one hand and negation on the other. The duality is one which characterises Lorca's work from the very outset, even in plays in which the outcome is not tragic. As far as aspiration is concerned, it may take many forms, be true of more than one character in a given play, and may also be extremely intense. In *Blood Wedding*, therefore, the aspiration of the Bride and Leonardo is for each other, while the Mother's aspiration is for the Bridegroom's happiness, but in each case it is intense to the point that the characters in question live in their own self-contained world, oblivious to all else. Or, to put it another way, individual aspiration is mutually exclusive.

In this context, it is clear that the Bride and Leonardo pursue very different ends from the Mother and the Bridegroom, as well, indeed, as the Bride's father. Moreover, the feelings and passions which make them aspire to those ends are ineradicable. The passion of the Bride and Leonardo for each other is not, in fact, new but goes back in time to when she was only fifteen, and is a deep-rooted attraction which the passage of time has failed to eradicate. In the same way the Mother's concern for her son's happiness is driven by her long-standing grief for her husband and elder son. In each case their course is set and cannot be changed, the die cast long before the commencement of the events we see on stage. When the Woodcutters of Act Three assert that 'You have to follow the blood's path', they are merely reinforcing the notion of things determined in advance, of the way things are. As the Mother observes in her final lament for the Bridegroom:

> On a day appointed, between two and three,
> The two men killed each other for love.

In terms of the response of the audience to the events placed before it in *Blood Wedding*, it is important to consider Lorca's even-handedness or moral objectivity in relation to his characters. We are made, in effect, not to judge the Bride but to see that, in spite of herself, she can do nothing about her attraction to Leonardo and therefore becomes the plaything of her passions, as indeed is the case with Leonardo himself. Similarly, as far as the Mother is concerned, we are made to understand that, despite her concern for her son, her hatred of the Félix family is such that she cannot stop herself sending him on what proves to be the fatal pursuit of Leonardo. In addition, the Bride, the Bridegroom, Leonardo and the Mother all have, in their different ways, positive characteristics. The Bride is young, physically attractive, anxious to please her father. The Bridegroom, though shy and naive, is loyal and affectionate. Leonardo, for all his faults, is handsome and passionate. And the Mother is fiercely loyal to her family, concerned about her son's future, and determined to uphold her reputation. In short, these are characters who invite sympathy and, precisely because of that, a deep sense of pity as we witness the destruction of everything to which they aspire. It is a sense of pity which is, moreover, intensified by our knowledge that they can do nothing to alter the course of events, once these have been set in motion. Indeed, by the end of the play pity could even be said to have become a feeling of fear and terror in the presence of such a remorseless process, which in turn places Lorca as a tragedian in the tradition of Sophocles and Euripides.

Production history

Spanish productions

The circumstances of Lorca's death in the first month of the Spanish Civil War aroused such feelings of shock and bitterness, not least in his own family, that his plays were not produced in

Spain during the first twenty years of the ensuing dictatorship. In both South America and in Europe his work was published, translated and performed. In France, for example, a translation of *Blood Wedding* by Marcelle Auclair and Jean Prévost, directed by Marcel Herrand, was presented in 1938 at the Théâtre de l'Atelier in Paris, and further translations of the play appeared in 1946, 1953 and 1956. Lorca's complete works, moreover, were first published not in Spain but in Buenos Aires in 1938. They were not published in Spain until 1954, eighteen years after Lorca's death, and productions of his plays did not take place until the early sixties when, in some respects, the Franco dictatorship began to relax its stranglehold.

The first major Spanish production of *Blood Wedding*, after Margarita Xirgu's staging of 1935, opened on 10 October 1962 at the Teatro Bellas Artes in Madrid. It was directed by José Tamayo, a distinguished name in Spanish theatre, with sets by José Caballero, and included in the cast Paquita Rico, José Luis Pellicena and Berta Riaza. The production, clearly very much in the spirit of Lorca's own concept of the play, was distinguished by its stylisation, as José Caballero's sketches and the production photographs suggest. The scene in the forest, for example, has as its background not naturalistic trees but highly stylised thorns which are, in effect, the visual equivalent of the Bride's words: 'What splinters of glass are stuck in my tongue!'

In the following year, on 4 May, a production of the play by the company of Maritza Caballero opened at the Teatro Barcelona in the Catalan capital, and almost a year later, on 17 April 1964, transferred to the Teatro Cómico in Madrid. In 1974 the dancer, Antonio Gades, produced his imaginative flamenco ballet version of the play, which, in 1981, became the basis of Carlos Saura's celebrated film. Five years later, fifty years after Lorca's death, the Spanish director, José Luis Gómez, brought his production for the Teatro de la Plaza to the Edinburgh International Festival, the very first time a Spanish production of the play had been staged in the United Kingdom. Writing in the *Financial Times* on 26 August 1986, Martin Hoyle drew attention to the stylisation of the set by Manfred Dittrich: '... three sides, plus lid, of a plain box, in unevenly applied brown wash. The back wall rises to reveal a sky of picture-postcard blue and two curved breast-like hills.' For Hoyle, however, such stylisation sat uneasily with the naturalistic aspects of the production, as it did for Eric Shorter in the *Telegraph*: 'Where the drama comes unstuck ... is in the effort to mingle the simple and realistic plot with the dramatist's metaphorical vision and choral commentaries.' In contrast, other critics reacted very positively. Michael Ratcliffe noted in the *Observer* that José Luis Gómez 'creates a rustic society whose rhythms are both formalised and spontaneous, gentle and fierce, in which speech, song and natural sound move in and out of one another without a break ... What a play!' And Joseph Farrell, in the *Scotsman*, concluded: 'What is especially admirable about this production is the balance between the solidity of peasant life and the intensity of the poetic scenes ... in spite of this earthiness, the poetry and poetic passages are given an intensity of their own. No other writer of our time, not even J. M. Synge to whom he is often compared, had Lorca's capacity to use poetry in the theatre to this effect, and no other director could give these pieces such an impact ...' Such different responses to Lorca's mixture of naturalism and stylisation, prose and poetry, suggest both how very personal critical reactions can be and, more importantly, the difficulty which *Blood Wedding* poses for any director.

US productions

One of the most interesting aspects of *Blood Wedding*'s production history in the USA is that it was performed there at such an early date and, to a certain extent, with assistance from Lorca himself. In November 1934 Irene Lewisohn, who in 1915 had with her sister Alice founded the Neighborhood Playhouse in New York, saw *Blood Wedding* in Spain and decided that she wished to present it in English translation in her own theatre. Translated by José Weissberger, an art expert who had lived for some time in Madrid, and with the title *Bitter Oleander*, the production opened at the Playhouse on 11 February 1935, the music arranged by Lorca himself. Mildred Adams (in *García Lorca: Playwright and Poet*, p. 172) has stated: '... the staging was handsome, the direction highly stylised. So was the acting. The whole passionate Spanish tragedy was played formally as masque, almost a ballet, with the translator's half Spanish, half English prose running through the action rather than dominating it. From time to time the audience, never really caught by the play's dramatic texture, laughed at an inept phrase. They found the Mother's passionate way of addressing her beloved son as "my carnation" merely funny...' Adams's observations do not, however, tell the whole story, for the production ran until March and some of the reviews recognised the quality of Lorca's play.

Although Lorca does not seem to have seen the New York production, his contribution to it was important not only in the sense that he arranged some of the music, but that in Madrid he had discussed aspects of it with Weissberger, who subsequently wrote marginal notes on several copies of his translation. These, combined with notes in the production's prompt-book, point very clearly to the importance which Lorca attached to music, as well as to the many choral passages in the play. In the New York production, therefore, background music was used for much of the wedding reception in Act Two, Scene Two, where there is such a complicated interplay of different voices. The scene began with guitar music, the Servant partly spoke and partly sang 'Turning,/ The wheel was turning...', the Bride and Bridegroom entered to the tune of 'Los cuatro muleros', and three more songs were used during the rest of the scene, the music ending abruptly with the news of the flight of the Bride and Leonardo.

Weissberger noted too that Act Three should be introduced, as had been the case in the Madrid production, by an 'andante of the Brandenburg Concerto of Bach', which is in fact the andante from the second of Bach's Brandenburg Concertos. Lorca's intention here was to prepare the audience for the highly poetic and stylised character of the forest scene with its non-human characters. In this context Bach's music may well have seemed to him to have the austere quality which he sought at this point in the play, and when he was writing it in 1932/33 he indeed listened a great deal to records of Bach's music.

The New York production also contained important changes in relation to the ending of Act Three, Scene Two, where the Wife begins the final elegiac tribute to the two dead men with 'He was a handsome horseman...', which is then taken up by the Mother, 'Sunflower to your mother...' Both these speeches were distributed amongst three neighbours against a background of chanting girls, a change which Weissberger notes was suggested by Lorca himself and which he did not introduce in the Madrid production on account of the poor quality of some of the actors. Finally, it seems that the speech of the Moon was omitted from the production because it was felt that it would hold up the action.

Subsequently, *Blood Wedding* would receive a number of important and interesting productions in the United States. In the early part of 1949, the translation by James Graham-Luján and Richard L. O'Connell was presented in New York by New Stages, an independent theatre company, at 159 Bleeker Street, directed by Bruno Tumarin. Writing in the *New York Times* in February, Brooks Atkinson enthused about the overall quality of the production, observing that 'The New Stages people have accepted the challenge and met it more than half way. This is just the sort of original, venturesome producing that Broadway rarely undertakes. Despite its imperfections, the performance of *Blood Wedding* is rich in poetic aspiration and deserves to be appreciated.' The set was clearly distinguished by its simplicity and adaptability, consisting of 'a sloping, uneven platform that captures the illusion of the Spanish countryside and needs only a prop or two to become the room of a house.' In turn, the starkness of the set was matched by acting which was 'gaunt and austere' and by movement which was 'spare' and economical. In particular, Brooks Atkinson picked out the performances of the actors who played Leonardo and the Bride: 'Alexander Scourby and Inge Adams are altogether excellent', though he also noted that 'Not all the actors have mastered the style as thoroughly as Mr Tumarin has in his direction'. In relation to the performance as a whole, the latter had 'attempted to orchestrate the parts like a piece of music'.

Three years later, in the autumn of 1952, *Blood Wedding* was produced at the Actors' Workshop in San Francisco, and again in the early part of 1958 at the Actors' Playhouse in New York, where it was directed by Patricia Newhall. Of the former, Dorothy Nichols commented in the *Palo Alto Times* on 27 December 1952 that 'once in a long while a play has such an impact that you want to leave the theater without speaking to anyone, without coming out from under its spell.' As for the New York production, Brooks Atkinson was again enthusiastic, concluding in the *New York Times* on 1 April 1958 that *Blood Wedding* is a work of 'terrible beauty'.

New York was once more the venue for the production by International Arts Relations Inc., in 1980, when the play was directed by Max Ferra, in an adaptation by María Irene Fornes, at 420 West 42nd Street. The approach in this case seems to have been largely 'realistic', according to Michiko Kakutani, who reviewed the production on 3 June in the *New York Times.* In the first two acts such an approach proved to be largely successful, but the third act clearly posed greater problems, for 'where García Lorca's surreal imagery becomes incarnate with two symbolic characters – the Moon (John Hilburn Wells) and the Beggar (Deanna Alida) – . . . Mr Ferra's essentially realistic approach begins to falter.' For this reviewer, who regarded both strong acting and strong directorial vision as essential to the play's performance, the acting left something to be desired, for it tended to be 'mannered and curiously lacking in passion. Consequently, there is much nervous staring into space where there should be anger, odd twitches of sentimentality where there should be dignity. It is almost as if the actors were embarrassed by the grand, almost primordial emotions of García Lorca's poetry.' On the credit side, the stark set suggested 'the very spiral of history with its steep curvature', while 'sensual lighting' enhanced the play's mood.

In 1988 *Blood Wedding* was produced at the Great Lakes Theater Festival, directed by Gerald Freedman in a translation by Michael Dewell and Carmen Zapata. It opened at the Ohio Theater in Cleveland on 8 October 1988 and on 9 December at the Coconut Grove Playhouse, Miami. Reviewing the production in the *Cleveland Plain Dealer*, Marienne Evett commented that the culture seemed alien but recognised that the spirit of Lorca's play was essentially that of Greek tragedy. For Norma Nuirka in the *Miami Herald* it seemed to be less a play than a staged poem. In the same newspaper, Christine Arnold found the sets striking, the lighting eerie and the costumes startling. On the other hand, the production seemed strangely unmoving, which she considered, at least in part, to be the fault of the translation which, for her, lacked 'the fluid beauty of Spanish'.

An acclaimed production of the play was presented in New York in 1992 where it was directed by Melia Bensussen at the Joseph Papp Public Theatre in a translation by Langston Hughes. Above all this production seems to have fused the different elements of the play, as Mel Gussow noted in the *New York Times* on 15 May: 'As directed by Ms Bensussen and as choreographed by Donald Byrd, the production merges both the naturalistic and metaphorical elements of the drama.' The design consisted of stuccoed walls and 'cycloramic strips of sky simulating the Spanish landscape'. In Act Three the surreal quality of the action was effectively paralleled by the set when the backdrop was transformed into a Miró-like landscape. For this reviewer, furthermore, the acting was particularly impressive. In the role of the Mother, Gloria Foster 'initially overdramatises her dialogue, but soon holds herself to García Lorca's pitch.' In the role of the Bride and Bridegroom, Elizabeth Peña and Al Rodrigo were 'evenly matched, in his resolute self-confidence and in her wishfulness, as she is seduced into a romance outside marriage. Joaquím de Almeida is a brooding Leonardo . . .'

British productions

The first British professional production of *Blood Wedding* appears to have taken place in 1954 at the Arts Theatre in London, directed by Peter Hall who used the American translation by Richard L. O'Connell and James Graham-Luján. Years later Harold Hobson (*Drama*, 2nd Quarter, 1981) referred to the production's stylisation and recalled in particular a scene in which 'Not a word was spoken. No character appeared. It was a scene in a woodland, and there was no sound or movement except a slight shiver of the bushes and the leaves on the trees. Yet there was present an extraordinary sense of evil, as there is sometimes in a story by Henry James. I noted it at the time as a most remarkable achievement.' The same translation as that used by Peter Hall also formed the basis of a production at the Nottingham Playhouse in March 1956, where it was directed by Kosta Spaic, of the Yugoslav National Drama Theatre. Subsequently, seventeen years were to pass before *Blood Wedding* was staged again, in February 1973 at the Leeds Playhouse, directed and translated by David Carson.

The fact that there were only three productions in almost twenty years is probably explained by the unfamiliarity of British directors and audiences with Lorca's work and the Spanish tradition in general, and by the frequent clumsiness of the O'Connell/Graham-

Luján translation, the 'authorised' translation at that time. 1986, on the other hand, marked the termination of the fifty-year copyright on the work published or first performed in Lorca's lifetime (though in 1995 this was reasserted for a further twenty years), and the appearance, therefore, of new translations of Lorca's plays which, in turn, led to many more productions and greater familiarity with his theatre in general.

The first of these productions, in the translation published here, was directed by Anthony Clark, with design by Nettie Edwards and music by Mark Vibrans, at the Contact Theatre, Manchester, in November 1987. Writing in the *Observer*, Michael Ratcliffe described the play as 'Lorca's great and under-performed masterpiece', presented 'in a tense well-designed production by Anthony Clark. Contact has one of the biggest open stages in the country. Clark uses it freely to convey the distancing of intimates and the closing of ranks.' Stylisation, rather than naturalism, was clearly the production's outstanding feature, be it in the arrangement and movement of characters, the speaking of the lines, or the settings in which the characters were located. Of the latter, Francesca Turner observed in the *Guardian*: '...Nettie Edwards' superb design uses bone shapes and skeletal bayonet branches, a skin-coloured backcloth with a cicatri hair in it, and primitive images of flowers and wool.' Particularly memorable aspects of the design were the great slash in the backcloth which in Acts One and Two assumed the visual form of the knife-wound feared by the Mother, and the bare branches which in Act Three, Scene One, pierced the back and side walls of the stage like the pointing fingers of fate as the Woodcutters rhythmically buried their axes in the stumps of trees. In this scene Mark Vibrans' eerie music also created a sense of both mystery and vastness, while the use of a multi-racial cast contributed greatly both to the play's sense of universality and its often unbearable emotional power.

Almost a year later a production of the play by Communicado Theatre Company, directed by Gerard Mulgrew, opened at the Lyceum Studio, Edinburgh, on 14 August and later transferred to the Donmar Warehouse, London. Using Scottish accents, seven actors were accompanied by two singers in a production again distinguished by its spareness and stylisation. For some the Scottishness of the play was a problem. Thus, Lyn Gardner in *City*

Limits noted that 'some of the performances remain primly Scottish (Alison Peebles' solid Bride is a case in point).' For others, including Joseph Farrell in the *Scotsman*, its Scottishness provided 'a context and a sense of felt experience, and from that base in reality the work can move beyond all periods and place.' Above all, the critics were impressed by the staging of the play which was both simple and inventive. In the wedding scene the guests silently mouthed their speeches. The actors, lined across the stage, imitated the sounds of nature, and at the end of the play a thin skein of blood-coloured wool was wound in to indicate the finality of the on-stage events. Joseph Farrell concluded that 'Communicado, under the direction of Gerard Mulgrew, has always been known for its willingness to mingle moods and to blend discordant styles, but never has their talent been put to better use than in their passionate, deeply felt, and brilliantly executed staging of Lorca's tragedy . . .'

A rather different production of *Blood Wedding*, directed by Jonathan Martin, and in a translation by Jonathan Martin and Mary Ann Vargas, was presented by the Asian Co-operative Theatre at the Half Moon Theatre, London, in October 1989. Naturally enough, the action on this occasion was given an Asian setting, which, for Nicholas de Jongh in the *Guardian*, made 'the rigidities and conventions of Lorca's peasants seem freshly appropriate', while the choral passages, sung rather than declaimed, 'no longer sound arch'. In general, though, de Jongh found that the production, which used 'a bald open space, with an occasional tree brought on', lacked 'erotic voltage and tension or devices to deal with the culminating symbolism'. Helen Rose, in *Time Out*, agreed that the staging 'only fleetingly captures the unique and fluid rhythms of Lorca's writing and fails to achieve the heights of a passion which surges with the sudden unstoppable force of a broken dam.' A quite different reaction, however, was that expressed by Alex Renton in the *Independent*, who found that 'Martin's sturdy, sure production is among the more convincing . . . Martin uses the width of the Half Moon stage to create an airy Andalusia of baked terracotta walls and cruel white light, an arena of suitable aridity for the gory tragedy. Performances are stark and precisely delineated . . . But the great pleasure is the pacing: from a disconcertingly leisured start the rush towards disaster is an obsessedly determined acceleration: the ritual of the wedding feast slips easily into the ritual of the hunt, the villagers brandishing their hoes and sickles like sacrificial knives...' Such diametrically opposed reactions illustrate very clearly the subjective nature of theatre reviews, which so often determine the fate of a particular production.

In December 1991, after a tour of the provinces, *Blood Wedding* received its most publicised production to date when it opened on the National Theatre's Cottesloe stage, directed by Yvonne Brewster and translated by Gwenda Pandolfi. The decision to set the play in Cuba and thus give the production a distinctly Afro-Caribbean character, was one which some critics saw as sensible, others as misguided. John Peter, in the *Sunday Times*, observed that 'Yvonne Brewster's production crosses the culture barrier with a daring stroke of imagination. Brewster herself was born in Jamaica and she has set the play in the Spanish Caribbean. The result is a brilliant sea change. We are in a recognisable rustic culture where singing and dancing can be a natural form of expression ... The Caribbean setting also solves a problem for anyone performing Lorca in English, which is the playing of his doom-laded lyricism, expressed in haunting surrealist images and fearfully poetic language. Brewster's cast translates much of this into boisterous but knowing humour, earthy, swaggering, menacing and flamboyant. The impact is both poetic and eerily disturbing: you sense the characters' fears, their savagely lyrical temperament, the primitive turbulence of their souls...' For others, including Martin Hoyle in the *Independent on Sunday*, the transposition weakened the play's impact, for 'Lorca's portrayal of a rigidly disciplined Spain where repressed passion chafes against the religious taboos and an honour-obsessed hierarchy is more than a hemisphere away from the relaxed physicality of the West Indies.' Amongst other things, the Caribbean setting demanded a stage design rather different from a production set in Andalusia, particularly in terms of landscape and vegetation, and in this regard the designer, Kendra Ullyart, introduced into her set branches which ended in red tropical blooms and orchids sprouting from sacks of grain. In addition, the Bride's home – a cave in Lorca's text – became an elongated bell-tent of white muslin, while some of the actors in the multi-racial cast wore white suits. As far as the playing was concerned – another aspect determined by the Caribbean setting – Claire Armistead, in the *Financial Times*, found fault with its tone: 'The mood is earthy, colloquial, even funny, but it does not offer a clear line through the poetic topsoil of the play.' For Paul Taylor in the *Independent*, the assumption of Spanish accents by some of the cast was a serious error: 'Since most of these would make Manuel in *Fawlty Towers* sound pedantically authentic, your involvement in the play keeps getting undermined by an inability to take what is being said seriously.' Amongst the critics there was, therefore, a variety of viewpoints which extended to almost every aspect of the production. To Rosalind Carne, in the *Guardian*, the 'entrance of the Moon with the Beggar Woman on his shoulders holding up her skirts looks silly', but for Paul Taylor, 'the Moon and Death, who lust for the lovers' blood and oversee their flight, are played with an unsettling, slightly childish exultancy by Peter Dineen and Anni Domingo . . . ' Taken as a whole, critical reaction to the National Theatre production reveals several important things: the problems involved in the transposition of a Lorca play to a setting other than Andalusia; the problems posed for actors, especially British actors, in performing Lorca; and, most of all perhaps, both the subjectivity of theatre critics in their judgement of productions of Lorca's plays, and their frequent ignorance of what is really required.

The staging of *Blood Wedding* by Julia Bardsley at the Haymarket Theatre, Leicester, in October 1992 in the translation published here, restored the location of the play to Spain and Andalusia in no uncertain fashion, notably through the use of a female flamenco singer. In addition, the play's final act was played in a bull-ring on which spectators looked down from tiered seats at the back of the stage. This said, the production largely ignored the stark simplicity demanded by Lorca in favour of visual style at the expense of language. Robin Thornber, in the *Guardian*, noted that: 'Julia Bardsley's production of this romantic tragedy of Spanish passion extends the boundaries of mainstream British theatre: the imagistic language she has evolved in studio and touring productions is now becoming established, but this is the most extreme example I've seen on the main stage of a major rep. This is the theatre of the nineties; we're catching up with the vivid allusiveness of pop video.' Some idea of the visual nature of the production may be suggested by the director's treatment of the

Woodcutters in Act Three, Scene One. Death, played here by a robed male figure, placed a travelling-bag centre-stage, opened it, reached inside, and slowly withdrew the handle of an axe, followed by, in turn, the three Woodcutters – a truly spectacular and astonishing moment. Acknowledging that 'dialogue doesn't take second place', Pat Ashworth in *Plays and Players* observed that '... it's the sights and sounds which capture the imagination. Shimmering, circling Ku Klux Klan-like figures create an aura of primitive superstition to herald the inevitable deaths. The Moon is a tragic figure, dancing intensely on pointe, urged on by Death with a whip. And the duel between Leonardo and the Bridegroom is fought out in slow motion in a blood-red arena, with Death wielding the knives and the crowd emitting the roar of the bullfight.' In presenting on stage Lorca's off-stage duel, and in having it performed in slow motion, Julia Bardsley was, of course, highly indebted to Carlos Saura's film adaptation of the play, which in turn reveals the visual emphasis of her production. Consequently, the performance ran for an hour longer than is normally the case.

The widely differing reactions of theatre critics to productions of *Blood Wedding* have already been noted, and can be seen once more in relation to its staging by Odyssey Theatre, in association with Cumbre Flamenca, at the Lyric Theatre, Hammersmith, London, in March–April 1993, directed by Nigel Jamieson. Framed by authentic flamenco song and dance, with the songs sung in Spanish, and with Helen Turner's design moving from initial realism to symbolism in the forest scene, the production delighted Michael Arditti in the *Evening Standard*: 'Nigel Jamieson's magnificent production at the Lyric revels in the exotic ... Helen Turner's design captures both the realistic and expressionistic elements of the play ... The performances are uniformly excellent...' In complete contrast, Irving Wardle in the *Independent on Sunday* referred, with a few exceptions, to 'an indifferent company' and saw the introduction of flamenco song and dance as contributing to 'a consciously exotic spectacle rather than a tragedy of common life'.

Claire Armistead began her review in the *Guardian* with the observation that '*Blood Wedding* is the earliest of Lorca's three great folk tragedies, and for my money the hardest to get right.' Most British theatre critics undoubtedly agree with her about

Lorca's greatness as a dramatist, and their differing reactions to the same production vividly illustrate the point that *Blood Wedding* is indeed hard to get right on a British stage. The fact remains, nevertheless, that, for me, the British productions discussed here have been more varied and challenging than any I have seen in Spain.

Translating Lorca

Translation of Lorca's work into English demands, firstly, considerable expertise in Spanish, and, secondly, familiarity with the 'world' which Lorca presents in his plays. In the case of the three rural tragedies, that 'world' is, of course, rural Andalusia, which is characterised by customs, traditions and beliefs very different from our own. The importance given to personal and family honour is an example of this – a cultural difference which the British always have great difficulty in understanding. In addition, the rural tragedies are full of allusions to the natural world which are either unfamiliar or embarrassing to the non-Spaniard, and especially to the city-bound northern European. Again, Lorca's work as a whole, poetry as well as drama, contains many images which have their roots in the popular imagination but which he developed in his own particular way. And finally, Lorca's style is extremely distinctive: his dialogue often remarkably spare and concise, his verse dense with images and resonance. For the translator, then, there are many pitfalls to avoid.

With regard to this translation of *Blood Wedding*, I have attempted to remain as close as possible to the original Spanish, for only by doing so is it possible to convey to the non-Spanish reader, spectator, or, indeed, actor or director, the essential Spanishness of the play, and to recreate the ordinary, everyday things which constitute the physical world in which the action and the characters of the play are set. On one level, this means that all the references to food, dress, flowers, plants, indeed to everything which is involved in creating the special 'world' of the play, must be translated exactly. An example occurs in Act One, Scene Three, when the father of the Bride boasts to the mother of the Bridegroom about his 'good crop of esparto'. At once, even though the esparto is never seen, the word conjures up a picture of the tough yellow grass which grows only in hot, dry climates, and thus evokes at the same time the desert land of Almería where the Bride lives with her father. Similarly, in the previous scene, the Wife's accusation that Leonardo has been seen 'the other side of the plains' by the 'women who pick capers' evokes both the geography of the area and the tasks of the peasant-women who live there. The text, then, is full of allusions to real, concrete objects – crops, weeds, stones – which, in Acts One and Two in particular, build a detailed picture of the physical character of the largely desert region of south-east Spain which Lorca knew so well and which is so different from other parts of Spain.

This world is also, of course, defined by particular traditions, to which there are frequent references in the play which must also be rendered faithfully. When in Act One, Scene Three, the Mother suggests to her future daughter-in-law that marriage means a husband, children and 'a wall that's two feet thick', the reference may seem strange, but it is important that the translation should not water it down, for the thickness of the walls suggests precisely the nature of a married woman's domestic and extremely curtailed life in the Spain of that time. Similarly, when just afterwards the Father offers refreshment to the Mother and the Bridegroom, he offers 'sweetmeats', not 'sweets' as it is sometimes translated, the word specifically suggesting a delicacy for a particular occasion. Again, the drink which the Wife gives to Leonardo in the previous scene should be rendered as 'lemon', not 'lemonade', for the drink consists of the natural juice of the lemon, to which water has been added.

Allusions by the characters to flowers are a difficult area, as was evident in the reaction of the audience to the New York production in 1935. Lorca's text contains many references to dahlias, carnations, roses, sunflowers and orange-blossom, many of them in association with particular individuals. So in Act One, Scene One, the Mother refers to her husband: 'He had the scent of carnation for me . . .', and just afterwards to her husband and her eldest son, both now dead: 'two men who were two geraniums . . .'. In the final scene of the play, she begins her lament to the now dead Bridegroom: 'Sunflower for your mother . . .'. British and American audiences, particularly those who live in cities, often cut off from

Nature, frequently find such allusions embarrassing, and it is not surprising that the New York audience in 1935 should have tittered on hearing them. Southern Europeans, on the other hand, are much more accustomed to thinking in that way, and in the context of the play nothing expresses better the beauty of human beings than images drawn from the beauty of Nature. In every case, therefore, Lorca's lines should be translated faithfully, for they reflect the psychology of the characters and the world to which they belong.

There is also in the Spanish tradition in general, and particularly in traditional Spanish poetry, a network of images to do with such things as oranges, lemons and the sea, which date back many centuries and which are therefore deeply embedded in the Spanish mentality. Sometimes occurring singly, sometimes in association with each other, they are to be found in poems dealing with love, in which the orange, the orange-tree and orange-blossom represent love's sweetness, the lemon and the lemon-tree love's bitterness, for which the sea with its bitter, salty water is another image. Lorca himself, thoroughly familiar with this tradition, frequently used its language to very telling effect. The 'drink of lemon' which the Wife gives Leonardo in Act One, Scene Two, becomes in this context, therefore, not simply something to quench his thirst, but also a pointer to the unhappiness and the bitterness felt by the Wife towards her husband, while his thirst is also his sexual thirst for the Bride. Similarly, in the wedding-songs of Act Two, Scene One, the Servant and the Third Girl have four significant lines which, in the light of the traditional meaning of the grapefruit (synonymous with the lemon) and the orange-tree, point to the Bride's restlessness and disquiet and the Bridegroom's naive optimism:

SERVANT. By the grape-fruit tree
The bride awake shall be.
THIRD GIRL (*entering*).
By the orange-grove
Spoon and cloth, his gifts of love.

These are good examples of the way in which Lorca incorporated traditional images into his own work and of the extent to which the translator and the reader need to be aware of that tradition and of Lorca's method.

Finally, it is important to recreate as far as possible the pattern and rhythm of Lorca's very distinctive language, and to avoid introducing additional words and phrases which would dissipate the energy of his writing. His dialogue is often remarkably austere, built on short phrases and repeated patterns which often reflect the obsessions of the characters. Such is the Mother's reply to her son in Act One, Scene One, when he tells her to stop talking about her dead menfolk:

> No. No vamos a acabar. ¿Me puede alguien traer a tu padre? ¿Y a tu hermano? Y luego, el presidio. ¿Qué es el presidio? ¡Allí comen, allí fuman, allí tocan los instrumentos! Mis muertos llenos de hierba, sin hablar, hechos polvo; dos hombres que eran dos geranios ... Los matadores, en presidio, frescos, viendo los montes ...

> No. I won't stop. Can someone bring your father back to me? And your brother? And then there's the gaol. What is the gaol? They eat there, they smoke there, they play instruments there. My dead ones full of weeds, silent, turned to dust; two men who were two geraniums ... The murderers, in gaol, as large as life, looking at the mountains ...

The verse passages of *Blood Wedding* naturally pose many problems for the translator, not least because they are often characterised not by rhyme but by assonance, of which the following song, with the first and then the alternate lines ending with the same stressed, unstressed 'a', is typical:

> Gir*a*b*a*,
> giraba la rueda
> y el agua pas*a*b*a*;
> porque llega la boda,
> se aparten las r*a*m*a*s
> y la luna se adorne
> por su blanca bar*a*nd*a*.

Although the same effect cannot be achieved in English, a mixture of rhyme and assonance can capture something of Lorca's original:

> Turning,
> The wheel was turning

And the water was flowing;
For the wedding-night's coming.
Let the branches now part
And the moon shine bright
On her balcony white.

Other verse passages present different problems, but in every case my aim in translating them has been to capture as far as possible both the meaning and the mood of the original in order to communicate the essential spirit of Spain's greatest twentieth-century dramatist.

Further Reading

Full-length studies on Lorca

Mildred Adams, *García Lorca: Playwright and Poet* (George Braziller, New York, 1977). An informal biography based on personal reminiscence.

Reed Anderson, *Federico García Lorca* (Macmillan, London, 1984). A useful study of Lorca's theatre as a whole.

Paul Binding, *Lorca: The Gay Imagination* (Gay Men's Press, London, 1985). An examination of Lorca's work from a gay perspective.

Manuel Durán (ed.), *Lorca: A Collection of Critical Essays* (Prentice Hall, New Jersey, 1962). Contains twelve essays on Lorca's poetry and theatre by academics and creative writers.

Gwynne Edwards, *Lorca: The Theatre Beneath the Sand* (Marion Boyars, London, 1980). A comprehensive study of Lorca's theatre which includes sections on staging.

Gwynne Edwards, *Dramatists in Perspective: Spanish Theatre in the Twentieth Century* (University of Wales Press, Cardiff, 1985). Chapter 3 examines Lorca in the context of European theatre.

Federico García Lorca, ed. Herbert Ramsden, *Bodas de sangre* (Manchester University Press, Manchester, 1980). This edition contains a very useful introduction to the play in English.

Federico García Lorca, ed. and trans. Christopher Maurer, *Deep Song and Other Prose* (Marion Boyars, London and Boston, 1980). A collection of articles and lectures by Lorca.

Francisco García Lorca, trans. Christopher Maurer, *In the Green Room: Memories of Federico* (Peter Owen, London, 1989). Contains reminiscences of theatre productions as well as analysis of plays.

Ian Gibson, *Federico García Lorca: A Life* (Faber and Faber, London, 1989). An authoritative study for anyone interested in Lorca's life and work.

Virginia Higginbotham, *The Comic Spirit of Federico García Lorca* (University of Texas Press, Austin, 1976). Concentrates on Lorca's theatre within the context of puppet-plays and farces.

Robert Lima, *The Theater of García Lorca* (Las Américas Publishing Co., New York, 1963). A detailed study with particular emphasis on fate.

Rafael Martínez Nadal, *Lorca's 'The Public': A Study of his Unfinished Play (El Público) and of Love and Death in the Work of Federico García Lorca* (Calder and Boyars, London, 1974). A wide-ranging and dense study of Lorca's work as a whole, including his most difficult play, *The Public*.

Andy Piasecki, *File on Lorca* (Methuen, London, 1991). One of the Methuen Writer-Files series. Contains synopses of Lorca's plays, as well as observations taken from various sources, including reviews of productions.

Jean J. Smoot, *A Comparison of Plays by John Millington Synge and Federico García Lorca: The Poets and Time* (Ediciones José Porrúa Turanzas, Madrid, 1978). Studies in particular the parallels between Lorca's three rural tragedies and some of the plays of Synge.

Articles and other studies

Reed Anderson, 'The Idea of Tragedy in García Lorca's *Blood Wedding*', *Revista Hispánica Moderna*, 38 (1974–5), pp. 174–88.

Robert Barnes, 'The Fusion of Poetry and Drama in *Blood Wedding*', *Modern Drama*, 2 (1960), pp. 395–402.

Ronald J. Dickson, 'Archetypal Symbolism in Lorca's *Bodas de sangre (Blood Wedding)*', *Literature and Psychology*, 10 (1961), pp. 76–9.

Gwynne Edwards, 'Lorca on the English Stage: Problems of Production and Translation', *New Theatre Quarterly*, 4, No. 16 (1988), pp. 344–55.

Ronald Gaskell, 'Theme and Form: Lorca's *Blood Wedding*', *Modern Drama*, 5 (1963), pp. 431–9.

Charles Lloyd Halliburton, 'García Lorca, the Tragedian: An Aristotelian Analysis of *Bodas de sangre*', *Revista de Estudios Hispánicos*, 2 (1968), pp. 35–40.

C. Brian Morris, *García Lorca: Bodas de sangre*, Critical Guides to Spanish Texts (Grant and Cutler Ltd, London, 1980).

Julian Palley, 'Archetypal Symbols in *Bodas de sangre*', *Hispania*, 50 (1967), pp. 74–9.

John T. H. Timm, 'Some Critical Observations on García Lorca's *Bodas de sangre*', *Revista de Estudios Hispánicos*, 7 (1973), pp. 255–88.

Eva K. Touster, 'Thematic Patterns in Lorca's *Blood Wedding*', *Modern Drama*, 7 (1964), pp. 16–27.

R. A. Zimbardo, 'The Mythic Pattern in Lorca's *Blood Wedding*', *Modern Drama*, 10 (1968), pp. 364–71.

Blood Wedding

Translated by Gwynne Edwards

This translation of *Blood Wedding* was first performed at the Contact Theatre, Manchester on 11 November 1987, with the following cast:

THE MOTHER	Maureen Morris
THE BRIDE	Sara Mair Thomas
THE MOTHER-IN-LAW/GIRL 2	Anni Domingo
THE NEIGHBOUR/THE SERVANT	Fenella Norman
THE WIFE OF LEONARDO	Charlotte Harvey
GIRL 1/DEATH (as a beggar woman)	Joan Carol Williams
LEONARDO	Tyrone Huggins
THE BRIDEGROOM	Ewen Cummins
THE FATHER OF THE BRIDE/THE MOON	Wyllie Longmore
YOUTH	Mark Crowshaw

WOODCUTTERS/GIRLS/GUESTS played by members of the Company

Directed by Anthony Clark
Designed by Nettie Edwards
Musical Director/Composer Mark Vibrans
Lighting by Stephen Henbest
Choreography by David Needham

Act One

Scene One

Room painted yellow.

BRIDEGROOM (*entering*). Mother.

MOTHER. What?

BRIDEGROOM. I'm going.

MOTHER. Where to?

BRIDEGROOM. To the vineyard. (*He starts to go out.*)

MOTHER. Wait.

BRIDEGROOM. Do you want something?

MOTHER. Son, your food.

BRIDEGROOM. Leave it. I'll eat grapes. Give me the knife.

MOTHER. What for?

BRIDEGROOM (*laughing*). To cut them.

MOTHER (*muttering and looking for it*). The knife, the knife ... Damn all of them and the scoundrel who invented them.

BRIDEGROOM. Let's change the subject.

MOTHER. And shotguns . . and pistols ... even the tiniest knife ... and mattocks and pitchforks ...

BRIDEGROOM. Alright.

MOTHER. Everything that can cut a man's body. A beautiful man, tasting the fullness of life, who goes out to the vineyards or tends to his olives, because they are his, inherited ...

BRIDEGROOM (*lowering his head*). Be quiet.

MOTHER. . . . and that man doesn't come back. Or if he does come back it's to put a palm-leaf on him or a plateful of coarse salt to stop him swelling. I don't know how you dare carry a knife on your body, nor how I can leave the serpent inside the chest.

BRIDEGROOM. Is that it?

MOTHER. If I lived to be a hundred, I wouldn't speak of anything else. First your father. He had the scent of carnation for me, and I enjoyed him for three short years. Then your brother. Is it fair? Is it possible that a thing as small as a pistol or a knife can put an end to a man who's a bull? I'll never be quiet. The months pass and hopelessness pecks at my eyes . . . even at the roots of my hair.

BRIDEGROOM (*forcefully*). Are you going to stop?

MOTHER. No. I won't stop. Can someone bring your father back to me? And your brother? And then there's the gaol. What is the gaol? They eat there, they smoke there, they play instruments there. My dead ones full of weeds, silent, turned to dust; two men who were two geraniums . . . The murderers, in gaol, as large as life, looking at the mountains . . .

BRIDEGROOM. Do you want me to kill them?

MOTHER. No . . . If I speak it's because . . . How am I not going to speak seeing you go out of that door? I don't like you carrying a knife. It's just that . . . I wish you wouldn't go out to the fields.

BRIDEGROOM (*laughing*). Come on!

MOTHER. I'd like you to be a woman. You wouldn't be going to the stream now and the two of us would embroider edgings and little woollen dogs.

BRIDEGROOM (*he puts his arm around his mother and laughs*). Mother, what if I were to take you with me to the vineyards?

MOTHER. What would an old woman do in the

vineyards? Would you put me under the vine-shoots?

BRIDEGROOM (*lifting her in his arms*). You old woman, you old, old woman, you old, old, old woman.

MOTHER. Your father, now he used to take me there. That's good stock. Good blood. Your grandfather left a son on every street corner. That's what I like. Men to be men; wheat wheat.

BRIDEGROOM. What about me, mother?

MOTHER. You? What?

BRIDEGROOM. Do I need to tell you again?

MOTHER (*serious*). Ah!

BRIDEGROOM. Do you think it's a bad idea?

MOTHER. No.

BRIDEGROOM. Well then?

MOTHER. I'm not sure. It's so sudden like this. It's taken me by surprise. I know that the girl's good. She is, isn't she? Well-behaved. Hard-working. She makes her bread and she sews her skirts. But even so, when I mention her name, it's as if they were pounding my head with a stone.

BRIDEGROOM. Don't be silly.

MOTHER. It's more than silly. I'll be left alone. Only you are left to me now and I'm sorry to see you going.

BRIDEGROOM. But you'll come with us.

MOTHER. No. I can't leave your father and your brother here. I have to go to them every morning, and if I leave, one of the Felixes could die, one of the family of murderers, and they'd bury him next to mine. I won't stand for that. Never that! Because I'll dig them up with my nails and all on my own I'll smash them to bits against the wall.

BRIDEGROOM (*strongly*). Back to that again!

MOTHER. I'm sorry. (*Pause.*) How long have you known her?

BRIDEGROOM. Three years. And now I've bought

the vineyard.

MOTHER. Three years. She had another young man, didn't she?

BRIDEGROOM. I don't know. I don't think so. Girls have to be careful who they marry.

MOTHER. Yes. I didn't look at anyone else. I looked at your father, and when they killed him I stared at the wall in front of me. One woman with one man, and there it is.

BRIDEGROOM. You know that my girl's good.

MOTHER. I don't doubt it. All the same, I'd like to know what her mother was like.

BRIDEGROOM. What's it matter?

MOTHER (*looking at him*). Son.

BRIDEGROOM. What do you want?

MOTHER. It's true. You're right. When do you want me to ask for her?

BRIDEGROOM (*happy*). Does Sunday seem alright?

MOTHER (*serious*). I'll take her the brass earrings, the really old ones, and you buy her . . .

BRIDEGROOM. But you know more . . .

MOTHER. You buy her some patterned stockings, and for yourself two suits . . . No. Three! I've only got you!

BRIDEGROOM. I'm going. I'll go and see her tomorrow.

MOTHER. Yes, yes, and see if you can make me happy with six grandchildren, or as many as you want, seeing your father didn't have a chance to give them to me.

BRIDEGROOM. The first one for you.

MOTHER. Yes, but let them be girls. Because I want to embroider and make lace and be at peace.

BRIDEGROOM. I'm sure you'll love my bride.

MOTHER. I will. (*She goes to kiss him but stops.*) Go on. You are far too big for kisses now. Give them to your wife. (*Pause. Aside.*) When she is your wife.

BRIDEGROOM. I'm going.

MOTHER. Dig the land by the little mill. You've been neglecting it.

BRIDEGROOM. It's settled then.

MOTHER. God go with you.

The BRIDEGROOM *leaves. The* MOTHER *remains seated, with her back to the door. A* NEIGHBOUR *appears at the door dressed in dark colours, a handkerchief on her head.*

Come in.

NEIGHBOUR. How are you?

MOTHER. You can see for yourself.

NEIGHBOUR. I came down to the shop so I've come to see you. We live so far from each other.

MOTHER. It's twenty years since I went to the top of the street.

NEIGHBOUR. You look well.

MOTHER. You think so?

NEIGHBOUR. Things happen. Two days ago they brought my neighbour's son home . . . both arms cut clean off by the machine. (*She sits down.*)

MOTHER. Rafael?

NEIGHBOUR. Yes. There it is. I often think your son and mine are better off where they are, sleeping, resting, no chance of being crippled.

MOTHER. Be quiet. It's all talk that, but there's no comfort in it.

They both sigh. Pause.

NEIGHBOUR (*sadly*). How is your son?

MOTHER. He's gone out.

NEIGHBOUR. He's bought the vineyard then!

MOTHER. He was lucky.

NEIGHBOUR. He'll get married now.

MOTHER (*as though waking up and drawing her chair to the* NEIGHBOUR*'s chair*). Listen.

NEIGHBOUR (*in a conspiratorial manner*). What is it?

MOTHER. Do you know my son's sweetheart?

NEIGHBOUR. A good girl!

MOTHER. Yes, but . . .

NEIGHBOUR. But there's no one knows her really well. She lives alone with her father out there, it's so far away, ten leagues from the nearest house. But she is good. She's used to solitude.

MOTHER. What about her mother?

NEIGHBOUR. Her mother, now I did know her. A good-looking woman. A glow on her face like a saint's; but I never liked her. She didn't love her husband.

MOTHER (*strongly*). Well, the things people get to know!

NEIGHBOUR. I'm sorry. I didn't mean to offend; but it's true. Now if she was respectable or not, no one ever said. No one ever mentioned that. She was proud.

MOTHER. It's always the same!

NEIGHBOUR. You did ask me.

MOTHER. I wish no one knew either of them – the girl or her mother. That they were like two thistles that no one dares name, and if you do they prick you.

NEIGHBOUR. You're right. Your son's precious.

MOTHER. He is. That's why I take care of him. They told me the girl had a young man some time ago.

NEIGHBOUR. She must have been fifteen. He got married two years ago now, to a cousin of hers in fact. No one remembers the engagement.

MOTHER. Why do you remember?

NEIGHBOUR. You do ask some questions!

MOTHER. Everyone likes to know about the things that hurt them. Who was the boy?

NEIGHBOUR. Leonardo.

MOTHER. Which Leonardo?

NEIGHBOUR. Leonardo, one of the Félix family.

MOTHER (*getting up*). The Félix family!

NEIGHBOUR. Woman, how can Leonardo be blamed

for anything? He was eight years old when those things happened.

MOTHER. I know . . . But I hear that name – Félix – and for me Félix is the same as filling my mouth with slime (*She spits.*) and I have to spit, I have to spit so it doesn't poison me.

NEIGHBOUR. Calm down. What good does it do you?

MOTHER. None. But you understand.

NEIGHBOUR. Don't stand in the way of your son's happiness. Don't tell him anything. You're an old woman. Me too. You and me, we have to keep quiet.

MOTHER. I won't say anything.

NEIGHBOUR (*kissing her*). Nothing.

MOTHER (*calmly*). Things! . . .

NEIGHBOUR. I'm going. My family will be back soon from the fields.

MOTHER. Have you ever seen such a hot day?

NEIGHBOUR. The children were fed up taking water to the harvesters. God be with you, woman.

MOTHER. God be with you.

The MOTHER *moves towards the door stage-left. Half-way there she stops and slowly crosses herself.*

Scene Two

A room painted pink, with copper ornaments and bunches of common flowers. Centre-stage, a table with a cloth. It is morning. LEONARDO*'s* MOTHER-IN-LAW *with a child in her arms. She rocks it. The* WIFE, *in the other corner, is knitting.*

MOTHER-IN-LAW. Lullaby, my baby sweet,
Of the great big stallion
Wouldn't drink the water deep.

There the water's oh so black,
Where the trees grow thick and strong.
When it flows down to the bridge,
There it stops and sings its song.

Who can say, my little one,
What the water's anguish is,
As he draws his tail along,
Through that nice green room of his.

WIFE (*quietly*). Go to sleep, carnation,
For the horse will not drink deep.

MOTHER-IN-LAW. Go to sleep, my little rose,
For the horse now starts to weep.

Horsey's hooves are red with blood,
Horsey's mane is frozen,
Deep inside his staring eyes
A silver dagger broken.

Down they went to the river bank,
Down to the stream they rode.
There his blood ran strong and fast,
Faster than the water could.

WIFE. Go to sleep, carnation,
For the horse will not drink deep.

MOTHER-IN-LAW. Go to sleep, my little rose,
For the horse now starts to weep.

WIFE. Horsey will not touch the bank,
Even though the bank is wet,
Even though his mouth is hot,
Streaming tiny drops of sweat.

To the mountains cold and hard,
He could only call and neigh,
Horsey's throat is hot and parched,
And the river bed is dry.

Oh, the great big stallion,
Wouldn't drink the water deep,
Pain as sharp as coldest ice,
Horse at break of day will weep.

MOTHER-IN-LAW. Don't come near. Stay outside.
Close the window, close it tight.
Weave a branch of finest dream,
Dream a branch so fine and light.

WIFE. Now my child is sleeping fast.

MOTHER-IN-LAW. Now my child will rest at last.

WIFE. Horsey, I would have you know,
Baby has a nice soft pillow.

MOTHER-IN-LAW. Baby's cradle made of steel.

WIFE. Baby's quilt so fine to feel.

MOTHER-IN-LAW. Lullaby, my baby sweet.

WIFE. Oh, the great big stallion,
Wouldn't drink the water deep.

MOTHER-IN-LAW. Don't come near, don't come in.
Seek the far off mountain.
Find the dark, the grey valley,
There the mare will waiting be.

WIFE (*looking*). Now my child is sleeping fast.

MOTHER-IN-LAW. Now my child will rest at last.

WIFE (*quietly*). Go to sleep, carnation,
For the horse will not drink deep.

MOTHER-IN-LAW (*rising and very quietly*).
Go to sleep, my little rose,
For the horse now starts to weep.

They take the child out. LEONARDO *enters.*

LEONARDO. Where's the baby?

WIFE. Fast asleep.

LEONARDO. He wasn't well yesterday. He cried in the night.

WIFE (*happy*). He's like a dahlia today. What about you?

Did you go to the blacksmith's?

LEONARDO. That's where I've come from. Would you believe? More than two months putting new shoes on the horse, and they always come off him. I reckon he rips them off on the stones.

WIFE. Couldn't it be you ride him a lot?

LEONARDO. No. I hardly ever ride him.

WIFE. Yesterday the neighbours told me they'd seen you the other side of the plains.

LEONARDO. Who said that?

WIFE. The women who pick capers. It surprised me, I can tell you. Was it you?

LEONARDO. No. What would I be doing over there, in that dry place?

WIFE. That's what I said. But the horse was half dead from sweating.

LEONARDO. Did you see him?

WIFE. No. My mother.

LEONARDO. Is she with the baby?

WIFE. Yes. Do you want a drink of lemon?

LEONARDO. With the water really cold.

WIFE. Not coming back to eat!

LEONARDO. I was with the wheat-weighers. They always hold people up.

WIFE (*making the drink, softly*). Do they pay a good price?

LEONARDO. Average.

WIFE. I need a dress. The baby needs a cap with ribbons.

LEONARDO (*getting up*). I'm going to see him.

WIFE. Take care. He's asleep.

MOTHER-IN-LAW (*entering*). So who's racing the horse like that? He's down there stretched out with his eyes bulging as if he's come from the end of the world.

LEONARDO (*sharply*). Me.

MOTHER-IN-LAW. Excuse me, he is yours.

WIFE (*timidly*). He was with the wheat-weighers.

MOTHER-IN-LAW. For all I care, he can burst. (*She sits down. Pause.*)

WIFE. The drink. Is it cold enough?

LEONARDO. Yes.

WIFE. Do you know they're asking for my cousin?

LEONARDO. When?

WIFE. Tomorrow. The wedding will be in less than a month. I expect they'll invite us.

LEONARDO (*seriously*). Who knows?

MOTHER-IN-LAW. I don't think his mother was very happy about the wedding.

LEONARDO. Perhaps she's right. That one needs watching.

WIFE. I don't like you thinking bad things about a good girl.

MOTHER-IN-LAW (*with malice*). When he says that it's because he knows her. Don't you know she was his girl for three years?

LEONARDO. But I left her. (*To his* WIFE.) Are you going to cry now? Stop it! (*He roughly pulls her hands from her face.*) Let's go and see the child.

They go out with their arms around each other. A GIRL *enters. She runs on happily.*

GIRL. Señora.

MOTHER-IN-LAW. What is it?

GIRL. The young man came to the shop and he bought all the best things.

MOTHER-IN-LAW. Was he alone?

GIRL. No. With his mother. Serious, tall. (*She imitates her.*) But very posh.

MOTHER-IN-LAW. They've got money.

GIRL. And they bought these fancy stockings! You should have seen them! The stockings women dream of! Look: a swallow here (*She points to her ankle.*), a boat there (*She points to her calf.*), and here a rose. (*She points to her thigh.*)

MOTHER-IN-LAW. Child!

GIRL. A rose with the seeds and the stalk! And all in silk!

MOTHER-IN-LAW. Two fortunes joined together.

LEONARDO *and his* WIFE *enter.*

GIRL. I've come to tell you what they're buying.

LEONARDO (*angrily*). We couldn't care less.

WIFE. Leave her.

MOTHER-IN-LAW. Leonardo, there's no need for that.

GIRL. Excuse me. (*She goes out weeping.*)

MOTHER-IN-LAW. Why do you have to upset people?

LEONARDO. I didn't ask for your opinion. (*He sits down.*)

MOTHER-IN-LAW. Very well. (*Pause.*)

WIFE (*to* LEONARDO). What's the matter with you? What's boiling away inside your head? Don't leave me like this, not knowing anything . . .

LEONARDO. Stop it!

WIFE. No. I want you to look at me and tell me.

LEONARDO. Leave me alone. (*He gets up.*)

WIFE. Where are you going?

LEONARDO (*sharply*). Can't you stop it?

MOTHER-IN-LAW (*forcefully, to her daughter*). Be quiet! (LEONARDO *leaves.*) The baby.

She goes out and reappears with the child in her arms. The WIFE *is still standing, motionless.*

Horsey's hooves are red with blood.
Horsey's mane is frozen.
Deep inside his staring eyes
A silver dagger broken.
Down they went to the river bank,
Down to the stream they rode.

There his blood ran strong and fast,
Faster than the water could.

WIFE (*turning slowly, as if in a dream*).
Go to sleep, carnation,
For the horse will now drink deep.

MOTHER-IN-LAW. Go to sleep, my little rose,
For the horse now starts to weep.

WIFE. Lullaby, my baby sweet.

MOTHER-IN-LAW. Oh, the great big stallion,
Wouldn't drink the water deep!

WIFE (*strongly*). Don't come near, don't come in.
Go away to the far-off mountain.
Oh, the pain is sharp as ice,
Horse of dawn that's breaking.

MOTHER-IN-LAW (*weeping*).
Now my child is sleeping fast.

WIFE (*weeping and slowly drawing closer*).
Now my child will rest at last.

MOTHER-IN-LAW. Go to sleep carnation,
For the horse will not drink deep.

WIFE (*weeping and leaning on the table*).
Go to sleep, my little rose,
For the horse now starts to weep.

Curtain

Scene Three

Interior of the cave where the BRIDE *lives. At the back a cross of big pink flowers. The doors are round with lace curtains and pink ribbon. On the walls, made of a white hard material, are round fans, blue jars and small mirrors.*

SERVANT. Please come in . . . (*She is pleasant, hypocritically deferential.*)

The BRIDEGROOM *and the* MOTHER *enter. The* MOTHER *is dressed in black satin and wears a lace mantilla. The* BRIDEGROOM *in black corduroy, wearing a chain of gold.*

Would you like to sit down? They'll be here soon.

She goes out. The MOTHER *and the* BRIDEGROOM *remain seated, stiff as statues. A long pause.*

MOTHER. Have you got your watch?

BRIDEGROOM. Yes. (*He takes it out and looks at it.*)

MOTHER. We have to get back in good time. These people live so far away!

BRIDEGROOM. But this land's good.

MOTHER. Yes, but too isolated. Four hours' journey and not a house or tree.

BRIDEGROOM. These are the dry lands.

MOTHER. Your father would have covered them with trees.

BRIDEGROOM. Without water?

MOTHER. He'd have looked for it. The three years he was married to me, he planted ten cherry trees. (*Recalling.*) Three walnut trees by the mill, a whole vineyard and a plant called Jupiter that has red flowers. But it dried up. (*Pause.*)

BRIDEGROOM (*referring to the* BRIDE). She must be getting dressed.

The FATHER *of the* BRIDE *enters, an old man with shining white hair. His head is bowed. The* MOTHER *and the* BRIDEGROOM *rise and they shake hands in silence.*

FATHER. Did the journey take long?

MOTHER. Four hours. (*They sit down.*)

FATHER. You must have come the longest way round.

MOTHER. I'm too old to cross the rough ground by the river.

BRIDEGROOM. It makes her giddy. (*Pause.*)

FATHER. A good crop of esparto.

BRIDEGROOM. Oh, very good.

FATHER. In my day this land didn't even produce esparto. I've had to punish it, even make it suffer, so it gives us something useful.

MOTHER. And now it does. Don't worry. I'm not going to ask you for anything.

FATHER (*smiling*). You are better off than me. Your vineyards are worth a fortune. Each vine-shoot a silver coin. What I'm sorry about is that the estates are . . . you know . . . separate. I like everything together. There's just one thorn in my heart, and that's that little orchard stuck between my fields, and they won't sell it to me for all the gold in the world.

BRIDEGROOM. It's always the same.

FATHER. If we could use twenty teams of oxen to bring your vineyards here and put them on the hillside. What a joy it would be!

MOTHER. But why?

FATHER. Mine is hers and yours his. That's why. To see it all together. Together, that would be a thing of beauty!

BRIDEGROOM. And it would be less work.

MOTHER. When I die, you can sell that and buy here next to this.

FATHER. Sell, sell! No! Buy, woman, buy everything. If I'd had sons, I'd have bought the whole of this hill right up to the stream. It's not good land; but with your arms you can make it good, and since no one passes by they don't steal the fruit and you can sleep easy. (*Pause.*)

MOTHER. You know why I've come.

FATHER. Yes.

MOTHER. So?

FATHER. I approve. They've talked it over.

MOTHER. My son has plenty, and he knows how to manage it.

FATHER. My daughter too.

MOTHER. My son's handsome. He's never known a woman. His name's cleaner than a sheet spread in the sun.

FATHER. What can I tell you about my girl? She's breaking up bread at three when the morning star's shining. She never talks too much; she's as soft as wool; she does all kinds of embroidery, and she can cut a piece of string with her teeth.

MOTHER. May God bless their house.

FATHER. May God bless it.

The SERVANT *appears with two trays. One with glasses and the other with sweets.*

MOTHER (*to the* SON). When would you like the wedding to be?

BRIDEGROOM. Next Thursday.

FATHER. The same day as her twenty-second birthday.

MOTHER. Twenty-two. That's what my son would have been if he were still alive. He'd be alive, warm, the true man that he was, if men hadn't invented knives.

FATHER. You mustn't dwell on that.

MOTHER. Every minute. Put your hand on your heart.

FATHER. Thursday then. Agreed?

BRIDEGROOM. Agreed.

FATHER. The bride and groom and we two, we'll go to the church in a carriage. It's a very long way. And the guests in the carts and on the horses they bring with them.

MOTHER. Agreed.

The SERVANT *comes in.*

FATHER. Tell her to come in now. (*To the* MOTHER.) I'll be very happy if you like her.

The BRIDE *enters. Her hands at her sides in a modest pose, her head bowed.*

MOTHER. Come! Are you happy?

BRIDE. Yes, señora.

FATHER. You mustn't be so serious. After all, she's going to be your mother.

BRIDE. I'm happy. When I say 'yes' it's because I want to.

MOTHER. Of course. (*She takes her by the chin.*) Look at me.

FATHER. She's like my wife in every way.

MOTHER. Is she? Such a lovely expression! You know what getting married is, child?

BRIDE (*solemnly*). I do.

MOTHER. A man, children, and as for the rest a wall that's two feet thick.

BRIDEGROOM. Who needs anything else?

MOTHER. Only that they should live. That's all . . . that they should live!

BRIDE. I know my duty.

MOTHER. Some gifts for you.

BRIDE. Thank you.

FATHER. Will you take something?

MOTHER. I'd rather not. (*To the* BRIDEGROOM.) Will you?

BRIDEGROOM. I will. (*He takes a sweetmeat. The* BRIDE *takes another.*)

FATHER (*to the* BRIDEGROOM.) Wine?

MOTHER. He doesn't touch it.

FATHER. That's good! (*Pause. They are all standing.*)

BRIDEGROOM (to the BRIDE.) I'll come tomorrow.

BRIDE. At what time?

BRIDEGROOM. At five.

BRIDE. I'll expect you.

BRIDE. When I leave your side I feel a great emptiness and a kind of lump in my throat.

BRIDE. When you are my husband you won't have it any more.

BRIDEGROOM. That's what I keep telling myself.

MOTHER. Let's go then. The sun doesn't wait. (*To the* FATHER.) Are we agreed on everything?

FATHER. Agreed.

MOTHER (*to the* SERVANT). Goodbye, woman.

SERVANT. God go with both of you.

The MOTHER *kisses the* BRIDE *and they begin to leave quietly.*

MOTHER (*at the door*). Goodbye, daughter.

The BRIDE *replies with a gesture.*

FATHER. I'll come outside with you.

They go out.

SERVANT. I'm bursting to see the presents.

BRIDE (*harshly*). Stop it!

SERVANT. Child! Show them to me!

BRIDE. I don't want to.

SERVANT. Just the stockings then. They say they're very fancy. Woman!

BRIDE. I said no.

SERVANT. For God's sake! Alright. It's as if you have no wish to get married.

BRIDE (*biting her hand in anger*). Oh!

SERVANT. Child, child! What's the matter? Are you sorry to be giving up this queen's life? Don't think of bitter things. There's no reason. None. Let's see the presents. (*She takes the box.*)

BRIDE (*gripping her by the wrists*). Let go.

SERVANT. Woman!

BRIDE. Let go, I said.

SERVANT. You're stronger than a man.

BRIDE. Haven't I done a man's work? I wish I was one.

SERVANT. Don't talk like that!

BRIDE. Shut up, I said. Let's talk about something else.

The light begins to fade. A long pause.

SERVANT. Did you hear a horse last night?

BRIDE. What time?

SERVANT. Three o'clock.

BRIDE. Probably a horse strayed from the herd.

SERVANT. No. It had a rider.

BRIDE. How do you know?

SERVANT. Because I saw him. He was standing by your window. It gave me a start.

BRIDE. Probably my young man. He's been here sometimes at that time.

SERVANT. No.

BRIDE. You saw him?

SERVANT. Yes.

BRIDE. Who was it?

SERVANT. It was Leonardo.

BRIDE (*forcefully*). That's a lie! A lie! Why should he come here?

SERVANT. He *was* here.

BRIDE. Be quiet! Damn your tongue.

The sound of a horse is heard.

SERVANT (*at the window*). Look! Come here! Was it him?

BRIDE. Yes, it was.

Quick curtain.

Act Two

Scene One

Entrance to the BRIDE*'s house. A large door in the background. Night. The* BRIDE *enters dressed in a white ruffled petticoat with lots of lace and embroidered edgings, and a white bodice. Her arms are bare. The* SERVANT *is similarly dressed.*

SERVANT. I'll finish combing your hair out here.

BRIDE. No one can stay inside there in this heat.

SERVANT. In these lands it doesn't get cool even at dawn.

The BRIDE *sits down on a low chair and looks at herself in a small hand-mirror. The* SERVANT *combs her hair.*

BRIDE. My mother came from a place where there were lots of trees. From a fertile land.

SERVANT. That's why she was full of joy.

BRIDE. She wasted away here.

SERVANT. Her fate.

BRIDE. Like we're all wasting away. The walls throw the heat out at us. Oh! Don't pull so hard.

SERVANT. It's to arrange this strand of hair better. I want it to come down over your forehead. (*The* BRIDE *looks at herself in the mirror.*) You do look beautiful! (*She kisses her with feeling.*)

BRIDE (*solemnly*). Just comb my hair.

SERVANT (*combing*). Such a lucky girl . . . to be able to put your arms around a man, to kiss him, to feel his weight!

BRIDE. Be quiet!

SERVANT. But it's best of all when you wake up and you feel him alongside you, and he strokes your shoulders with his breath, like a nightingale's feather.

BRIDE (*forcefully*). Will you be quiet!

SERVANT. But child! What is marriage? That's what marriage is. Nothing more! Is it the sweetmeats? Is it the bunches of flowers? Of course it's not! It's a shining bed and a man and a woman.

BRIDE. You shouldn't talk about such things.

SERVANT. That's another matter. But there's plenty of pleasure!

BRIDE. Or plenty of bitterness.

SERVANT. I'm going to put the orange-blossom from here to here, so that the wreath will crown your hair. (*She tries on the sprigs of orange-blossom.*)

BRIDE (*she looks at herself in the mirror*). Give it to me. (*She takes the orange-blossom, looks at it and lowers her head dejectedly.*)

SERVANT. What's the matter?

BRIDE. Leave me alone!

SERVANT. It's no time to be feeling sad. (*Spiritedly.*) Give me the orange-blossom. (*The* BRIDE *throws the wreath away.*) Child! Don't tempt fate by throwing the flowers on the floor! Look at me now. Don't you want to get married? Tell me. You can still change your mind. (*She gets up.*)

BRIDE. Dark clouds. A cold wind here inside me. Doesn't everyone feel it?

SERVANT. Do you love your young man?

BRIDE. I love him.

SERVANT. Yes, yes, of course you do.

BRIDE. But it's a very big step.

SERVANT. It has to be taken.

BRIDE. I've already agreed to take it.

SERVANT. I'll fix the wreath for you.

BRIDE (*she sits down*). Hurry, they must be almost here.

SERVANT. They'll have been on the road at least two hours.

BRIDE. How far is it from here to the church?

SERVANT. Five leagues if you go by the stream. If you take the road it's twice as far.

The BRIDE *gets up and the* SERVANT *is excited as she observes her.*

Oh let the bride awaken now
On this her wedding day.
Oh let the rivers of the world
Now bear your bridal-crown away.

BRIDE (*smiling*). Come on.

SERVANT (*she kisses her with feeling and dances around her.*)

Oh let the bride awaken now
To sprig of flowering laurel green.
Oh let the bride awaken now
And by the laurel trees be seen!

A loud knocking is heard.

BRIDE. Open it. It must be the first of the guests. (*She goes out.*)

The SERVANT *opens the door. She is startled.*

SERVANT. You?

LEONARDO. Me. Good morning.

SERVANT. The very first to arrive!

LEONARDO. Haven't I been invited then?

SERVANT. Yes.

LEONARDO. So I'm here.

SERVANT. Where's your wife?

LEONARDO. I came on horseback. She's coming by road.

SERVANT. Did you meet anyone else?

LEONARDO. I rode past them.

SERVANT. You'll kill the animal racing him like that.

LEONARDO. If he dies, he dies!

Pause.

SERVANT. Sit yourself down. There's no one up yet.
LEONARDO. Where's the bride?
SERVANT. I'm going to dress her this very minute.
LEONARDO. She'll be happy I expect! The bride!
SERVANT (*changing the subject*). How's the child?
LEONARDO. Child?
SERVANT. Your little son.
LEONARDO (*recalling, as if in a dream*). Ah!
SERVANT. Is he coming with them?
LEONARDO. No.

Pause. Voices singing in the distance.

VOICES. Let the bride awaken now
On this her wedding day.
LEONARDO. Let the bride awaken now
On this her wedding day.
SERVANT. It's the guests. Still a long way off.
LEONARDO (*getting up*). I suppose the bride will be wearing a big wreath of flowers? It shouldn't be so big. Something smaller would suit her better. Did the bridegroom bring the orange-blossom so she can wear it on her heart?
BRIDE (*she appears still in petticoats and with the wreath of flowers in place*). He brought it.
SERVANT (*strongly*). Don't come out like that.
BRIDE. What's the matter? (*Seriously.*) Why do you want to know if they brought the orange-blossom? What are you hinting at?
LEONARDO. What would I be hinting at? (*Moving closer.*) You, you know me, you know I'm not hinting. Tell me. What was I to you? Open up your memory, refresh it. But two oxen and a broken-down shack are almost nothing. That's the thorn.
BRIDE. Why have you come?
LEONARDO. To see your wedding.

BRIDE. I saw yours too!

LEONARDO. You fixed that, you made it with your own two hands. They can kill me, but they can't spit on me. Now silver, shine as it may, can often spit.

BRIDE. That's a lie.

LEONARDO. I don't want to speak out. I'm a man of honour and I don't want all these hills to have to listen to my complaints.

BRIDE. Mine would be louder.

SERVANT. This argument mustn't go on. You mustn't talk about what's gone. (*The* SERVANT *looks anxiously towards the doors.*)

BRIDE. She's right. I shouldn't even be talking to you. But it makes my blood boil that you should come to watch me and spy on my wedding and make insinuations about the orange-blossom. Go and wait for your wife outside.

LEONARDO. Can't we talk, you and me?

SERVANT (*angrily*). No: you can't talk.

LEONARDO. From the day of my wedding I've thought night and day about whose fault it was, and every time I think I find another fault that eats the old one up, but it's always someone's fault!

BRIDE. A man with a horse knows many things and can do a lot to take advantage of a girl abandoned in a desert. But I've got my pride. Which is why I'm getting married. And I'll shut myself away with my husband, and I'll love him above everything.

LEONARDO. Pride will get you nowhere! (*He approaches her.*)

BRIDE. Don't come near me!

LEONARDO. To keep quiet and burn is the greatest punishment we can heap upon ourselves. What use was pride to me and not seeing you and leaving you awake night after night? No use! It only brought the fire down on top of me! You think that time heals and walls conceal, and it's not true, not true! When the roots of things go deep, no one can pull them up!

BRIDE (*trembling*). I can't hear you. I can't hear your voice. It's as if I'd drunk a bottle of anise and fallen asleep on a bedspread of roses. And it drags me along, and I know that I'm drowning, but I still go on.

SERVANT (*seizing* LEONARDO *by the lapels*). You should leave now!

LEONARDO. It's the last time I'm going to speak to her. There's nothing to be afraid of.

BRIDE. And I know I'm mad, and I know that my heart's putrified from holding out, and here I am, soothed by the sound of his voice, by the sight of his arms moving.

LEONARDO. I won't be at peace with myself if I don't tell you all this. I got married. You get married now!

SERVANT (*to* LEONARDO). She will!

VOICES (*singing nearer*).

Oh let the bride awaken now
On this her wedding day!

BRIDE. Let the bride awaken!

She runs out to her room.

SERVANT. The guests are here. (*To* LEONARDO.) Don't you go near her again.

LEONARDO. Don't worry.

He goes out stage-left. It starts to get light.

FIRST GIRL (*entering*).

Let the bride awaken now
On this her wedding day;
Begin the dance, let flowers now
Your balconies array.

VOICES. Let the bride awaken!

SERVANT (*whipping up enthusiasm*).
Let the bride awaken
To the bright display
Of love's rich green bouquet.
May she awaken now
To trunk and flowering bough
Of laurel on her wedding day.
SECOND GIRL (*entering*).
Let her awaken.
Her long hair covers her throat.
White as snow is her petticoat.
Leather and silver on her feet.
Head adorned by jasmine sweet.
SERVANT. Oh, shepherd-girl,
The moon appears above.
FIRST GIRL. Oh, handsome lad,
Leave your hat in the olive grove.
FIRST YOUTH (*enters, holding aloft his hat*).
Let the bride awaken
To welcome the wedding-guests.
Through distant fields they move ahead.
Trays of dahlias are their gifts,
Loaves of consecrated bread.
VOICES. May the bride awaken!
SECOND GIRL. The bride
Puts on her crown of flowers.
The groom
Secures it with golden ribbons.
SERVANT. By the grape-fruit tree
The bride awake shall be.
THIRD GIRL (*entering*).
By the orange-grove
Spoon and cloth, his gifts of love.

Three GUESTS *enter.*

FIRST YOUTH. Sweet dove, awaken!
The dawn scrubs bright
The shadowy bells of night.
GUEST. Bride, oh fair white bride,
Today a maiden she.
Tomorrow a wife shall be.
FIRST GIRL. Come down, dark girl,
Trail behind your silken train.
GUEST. Come down, little dark one,
For morning dew's like icy rain.
FIRST YOUTH. Awaken, bride, awaken.
Orange-blossom the breeze shall stain.
SERVANT. A tree I shall embroider,
Adorned with ribbons of darkest red.
On every one a child, and this:
'Long life to them when they are wed.'
VOICES. Let the bride awaken!
FIRST YOUTH. On this her wedding day!
GUEST. On this your wedding day
How handsome you shall be.
True flower of the mountain,
Wife of a captain worthy.
FATHER (*entering*). Wife of a true captain,
The bridegroom takes her with him.
He comes to claim his treasure,
Accompanied by oxen.
THIRD GIRL. The bridegroom
Is a golden flower.
With every step
Carnations shower.
SERVANT. Oh, lucky child!
SECOND YOUTH. Let the bride awaken.
SERVANT. Oh, lovely bride!
FIRST GIRL. The wedding
From every window calls.

SECOND GIRL. Let the bride appear.
FIRST GIRL. Let the bells ring,
Let the bells shout!
FIRST YOUTH. She comes! The bride is here.
SERVANT. Like a great bull, the wedding
Begins to stir.

The BRIDE *appears. She wears a black dress in the style of 1900, with a bustle and a long train of pleated gauze and heavy lace. On her hair, which falls across her forehead, she wears a wreath of orange-blossom. The sound of guitars. The* GIRLS *kiss the* BRIDE.

THIRD GIRL. What perfume did you put on your hair?
BRIDE (*laughing*). None.
SECOND GIRL (*looking at her dress*). The material's wonderful!
FIRST YOUTH. Here's the bridegroom!
BRIDEGROOM. Welcome!
FIRST GIRL (*placing a flower behind his ear*).
The bridegroom
Is a golden flower.
SECOND GIRL. His eyes communicate
His joy to ours.

The BRIDEGROOM *goes over to the* BRIDE.

BRIDE. Why did you put those shoes on?
BRIDEGROOM. They look more cheerful than the black ones.
LEONARDO'S WIFE (*entering and kissing the* BRIDE). Good health!

Everyone chatters excitedly.

LEONARDO (*entering like someone performing a duty*).
On your wedding day
This crown you shall wear.

WIFE. So the fields will be gladdened
With the dew of your hair.

MOTHER (*to the* FATHER). Are they here too?

FATHER. They are family. Today's a day for forgiveness.

MOTHER. I'll put up with it but I shan't forgive.

BRIDEGROOM. With the crown it's a joy to look at you!

BRIDE. Let's get to the church quickly.

BRIDEGROOM. Why the hurry?

BRIDE. I want to be your wife and be alone with you and not hear any other voice but yours.

BRIDEGROOM. That's what I want!

BRIDE. And to see only your eyes. And to have you hold me so tight that, even if my mother were to call me, my dead mother, I couldn't free myself from you.

BRIDEGROOM. My arms are strong. I'm going to hold you for forty years without stopping.

BRIDE (*dramatically, taking his arms*). For ever!

FATHER. Let's go quickly! Bring the horses and the carts! The sun has risen.

MOTHER. Drive carefully. Let's hope nothing goes wrong.

The great door opens back-stage. They begin to leave.

SERVANT (*crying*). When you leave your home,
Oh maiden white,
Remember you leave,
A star shining bright.

FIRST GIRL. Clean your body, clean your dress.
Leaving home, bride to be blessed.

They continue leaving.

SECOND GIRL. Leaving your home
For the church's blessing!

SERVANT. The breeze in sand
bright flowers leaves!

THIRD GIRL. Oh, white young girl!

SERVANT. Dark breeze the lace
Of her mantilla weaves.

They leave. Guitars, castanets and tambourines are heard. LEONARDO *and his* WIFE *are left alone.*

WIFE. Let's go.

LEONARDO. Where to?

WIFE. To the church. But you aren't going on horseback. You are coming with me.

LEONARDO. In the cart?

WIFE. How else?

LEONARDO. I'm not the kind of man to go by cart.

WIFE. And I'm not the kind of woman to go to a wedding without her husband. I can't put up with it any more!

LEONARDO. Neither can I!

WIFE. Why are you looking at me like that? A thorn in each eye!

LEONARDO. Let's go.

WIFE. I don't know what's happening. But I think and I don't want to think. One thing I do know. I've already been thrown aside. But I've got a child. And another one coming. It's the way things are. My mother's fate was the same. But I won't be moved from here. (*Voices off.*)

VOICES. When you leave your home
For the church's blessing,
Remember you leave
Like a bright star shining!

WIFE (*weeping*). Remember you leave,
A bright star shining
That's how I left my house too. The whole world was mine.

LEONARDO (*getting up*). Let's go.

WIFE. But with me!

LEONARDO. Yes. (*Pause.*) Come on then! (*They go out.*)

VOICES. When you leave your home
For the church's blessing,
Remember you leave
Like a bright star shining.

Slow curtain.

Scene Two

Outside the BRIDE*'s cave. Interplay of grey, white, and cold blues. Large prickly pears. Dark and silver tones. Background of plains the colour of biscuit, and everything hard as if it were a landscape in popular ceramic.*

SERVANT (*arranging glasses and trays on a table*).
Turning,
The wheel was turning
And the water was flowing;
For the wedding-night's coming.
Let the branches now part,
And the moon shine bright
On her balcony white.

(*Loudly.*) Put out the tablecloths.

(*In a poetic voice.*) Singing,
Bride and groom singing,
And the water was flowing;
For the wedding-night's coming.
See the frost's cold brightness.
Let the almond's bitterness
Be honey's sweetness.

(*Loudly.*) Get the wine ready.

(*In a poetic voice.*) Lovely girl,
Oh, loveliest of all.
See the water flowing,
For your wedding-night's coming.
Pull your skirts in tight,
Hide beneath your husband's wing
And never leave him.
For your husband's a dove
Whose breast is burning,
As the fields are waiting
For fresh blood running.
Turning,
The wheel was turning
And the water was flowing.
Your wedding-night's coming
And the water's gleaming.

MOTHER (*entering*). At last!

FATHER. Are we the first?

SERVANT. No. It's a while since Leonardo got here with his wife. They drove like demons. The wife was dead with fright. They made the journey as if they'd come on horseback.

FATHER. That one looks for trouble. He hasn't got good blood.

MOTHER. What blood could he have? The blood of his entire family. It comes from his great-grandfather, who started the killing, and it spreads through the whole breed, all of them knife-handlers and smiling hypocrites.

FATHER. Let's leave it!

SERVANT. How can she leave it?

MOTHER. It hurts to the ends of my veins. On the face of every one of them I can only see the hand that killed what was mine. Do you see me? Do I seem mad to you? Well I am mad from not being able to shout what my heart demands. There's a scream here in my heart that's always rising up, and I have to force it down again and hide it in these shawls. They've taken my dead ones from me and I have to be silent. And because of that people criticize. (*She removes her shawl.*)

FATHER. Today's no day to remember those things.

MOTHER. When I start to talk, I have to speak out. And today even more. Because today I'm left alone in my house.

FATHER. In the hope of having company.

MOTHER. That is my hope: grandchildren. (*They sit.*)

FATHER. I want them to have many. This land needs arms that are not paid for. You have to wage a constant battle with the weeds, with the thistles, with the stones that come up from who knows where. And these arms must belong to the owners, so that they can punish and master, so that they can make the seed flourish. Many sons are needed.

MOTHER. And some daughters! Men are like the wind. In the nature of things they have to handle weapons. Girls never go into the street.

FATHER (*happily*). I think they'll have both.

MOTHER. My son will cover her well. He's of good seed. His father could have had many sons with me.

FATHER. What I'd like is that this should happen in a single day. That straight away they should have two or three boys.

MOTHER. But it's not like that. It takes a long time. That's why it's so terrible to see your blood spilt on the ground. A fountain that spurts for a minute and has cost us years. When I reached my son, he was lying in the middle of the road. I wet my hands with his blood and I licked them with my tongue. Because it was mine. You don't know what that means. I'd put the earth soaked by it in a monstrance of glass and topaz.

FATHER. There's something to hope for now. My

daughter's wide-hipped and your son's strong.

MOTHER. So I'm hoping. (*They rise.*)

FATHER. Get the trays of wheat ready.

SERVANT. They are ready.

LEONARDO'S WIFE (*entering*). Good luck for the future!

MOTHER. Thank you.

LEONARDO. Is there going to be a celebration?

FATHER. A small one. The people can't stay for long.

SERVANT. Here they are!

The GUESTS *enter in happy groups. The* BRIDAL COUPLE *enter arm in arm.* LEONARDO *leaves.*

BRIDEGROOM. There was never a wedding with so many people.

BRIDE (*darkly*). Never.

FATHER. It was magnificent.

MOTHER. Whole branches of families were there.

BRIDEGROOM. People who never went out of the house.

MOTHER. Your father sowed the seed. Now you reap the harvest.

BRIDEGROOM. There were cousins of mine I didn't even know.

MOTHER. All the people from the coast.

BRIDEGROOM (*happily*). They were scared of the horses. (*They talk.*)

MOTHER (*to the* BRIDE). What are you thinking?

BRIDE. Nothing.

MOTHER. Your blessings weigh heavily. (*Guitars are heard.*)

BRIDE. Like lead.

MOTHER (*strongly*). But they shouldn't. You should be as light as a dove.

BRIDE. Are you staying here tonight?

MOTHER. No. My house is empty.

BRIDE. You ought to stay!

FATHER (*to the* MOTHER). Look at the dance they are forming. Dances from the seashore right over there.

LEONARDO *enters and sits down. His* WIFE *is behind him, standing stiffly.*

MOTHER. They are my husband's cousins. As hard as stones when it comes to dancing.

FATHER. It's a joy to see them. What a change for this house! (*He leaves.*)

BRIDEGROOM (*to the* BRIDE). Did you like the orange-blossom?

BRIDE (*looking at him fixedly*). Yes.

BRIDEGROOM. It's all made of wax. It'll last for ever. I'd like you to have worn them all over your dress.

BRIDE. There's no need for that.

LEONARDO *goes off to the right.*

FIRST GIRL. We'll take your pins out.

BRIDE (*to the* BRIDEGROOM). I'll be back in a minute.

WIFE. I hope you'll be happy with my cousin!

BRIDEGROOM. I'm sure I will.

WIFE. The two of you here; never going out, building a home. I wish I lived as far away as this.

BRIDEGROOM. Why don't you buy land? The mountain's cheap and it's better for bringing up children.

WIFE. We've got no money. And the way we are going!

BRIDEGROOM. Your husband's a good worker.

WIFE. Yes, but he likes to fly around too much. From one thing to another. He's not a steady person.

SERVANT. Aren't you having anything? I'll wrap some wine-cakes for your mother. She really likes them.

BRIDEGROOM. Give her three dozen.

WIFE. No, no. Half a dozen will be quite enough.

BRIDEGROOM. It's a special day.

WIFE (*to the* SERVANT). Where's Leonardo?

SERVANT. I haven't seen him.

BRIDEGROOM. He must be with the guests.

WIFE. I'll go and see. (*She leaves.*)

SERVANT. That's beautiful.

BRIDEGROOM. Aren't you dancing?

SERVANT. There's no one will dance with me.

Two GIRLS *pass across the background; during the entire scene the background will be a lively interplay of figures.*

BRIDEGROOM (*happy*). That's because they don't understand. Lively old women like you dance better than young girls.

SERVANT. Are you trying to flirt with me, boy? What a family you are! Men amongst men! When I was a child I saw your grandfather. What a man! As if a mountain was getting married!

BRIDEGROOM. I'm not as big as that.

SERVANT. But the same twinkle in your eyes. Where's the girl?

BRIDEGROOM. Taking off her head-dress.

SERVANT. Look! For the middle of the night, since you won't be sleeping, I've prepared some ham, and some big glasses of old wine. In the bottom part of the cupboard. Just in case you need it.

BRIDEGROOM. I don't eat in the middle of the night.

SERVANT (*teasing*). If you don't, your wife then. (*She goes out.*)

FIRST YOUTH (*entering*). You've got to have a drink with us.

BRIDEGROOM. I'm waiting for my wife.

SECOND YOUTH. You'll have her in the early hours.

FIRST YOUTH. When it's best!

SECOND YOUTH. Only for a minute!

BRIDEGROOM. Alright.

They leave. Sounds of great excitement. The BRIDE *appears. From the opposite side two* GIRLS *run to meet her.*

FIRST GIRL. Who did you give the first pin to? Me or her?

BRIDE. I don't remember.

FIRST GIRL. You gave it to me here.

SECOND GIRL. You gave it to me, in front of the altar.

BRIDE (*uneasy, with a sense of great inner conflict*). I don't know.

FIRST GIRL. I wish you'd . . .

BRIDE (*interrupting*). And I don't care. I've got lots of things on my mind.

SECOND GIRL. I'm sorry.

LEONARDO *crosses the back-stage.*

BRIDE (*she sees* LEONARDO). And it's a difficult time!

FIRST GIRL. Well, we don't know!

BRIDE. You'll know when your time comes. It's a difficult step to take.

FIRST GIRL. Are you angry?

BRIDE. No. I'm sorry.

SECOND GIRL. What for? But the two pins are for getting married, right?

BRIDE. Both of them.

FIRST GIRL. We'll see which one of us gets married first.

BRIDE. Are you so anxious?

SECOND GIRL (*coyly*). Yes.

BRIDE. But why?

FIRST GIRL. Well . . . (*Embracing the second girl.*)

They run away. The BRIDEGROOM *enters slowly and embraces the* BRIDE *from behind.*

BRIDE (*very startled*). Don't.

BRIDEGROOM. Are you frightened of me?

BRIDE. Oh! It's you!

BRIDEGROOM. Who else? (*Pause.*) Me or your father.

BRIDE. Yes.

BRIDEGROOM. Though your father would have hugged you more gently.

BRIDE (*gloomily*). Yes.

BRIDEGROOM. Because he's old. (*He embraces her strongly and a bit roughly.*)

BRIDE (*curtly*). Stop it!

BRIDEGROOM. Why? (*He releases her.*)

BRIDE. Well . . . the guests. They can see us.

The SERVANT *crosses back-stage again, without looking at the* BRIDE *and* BRIDEGROOM.

BRIDEGROOM. So? We've taken our vows.

BRIDE. Yes, but leave me be . . . Now.

BRIDEGROOM. What's the matter? It's as if you are frightened.

BRIDE. It's nothing. Don't go.

LEONARDO'*s* WIFE *enters.*

WIFE. I don't mean to interrupt . . .

BRIDE. What is it?

WIFE. Did my husband come through here?

BRIDEGROOM. No.

WIFE. It's just that I can't find him, and the horse isn't in the stable.

BRIDEGROOM (*happily*). He's probably gone for a ride.

The WIFE *goes out, disturbed. The* SERVANT *enters.*

SERVANT. Aren't you pleased with all these good wishes?

BRIDEGROOM. I want it to be over and done with. My wife's a bit tired.

SERVANT. What's the matter, child?

BRIDE. It's as if someone's struck me on the head!

SERVANT. A bride from these mountains has to be strong. (*To the* BRIDEGROOM.) You are the only one who can cure her, since she's yours. (*She runs out.*)

BRIDEGROOM (*embracing her*). Let's go and dance for a bit. (*He kisses her.*)

BRIDE (*disturbed*). No. I want to lie down on the bed.

BRIDEGROOM. I'll come with you.

BRIDE. No! Not with all these people here! What would they say? Let me rest for a moment.

BRIDEGROOM. Whatever you want. But don't be like this tonight!

BRIDE (*at the door*). I'll be better tonight.

BRIDEGROOM. I hope you will.

The MOTHER *enters.*

MOTHER. Son.

BRIDEGROOM. Where've you been?

MOTHER. In the middle of all that noise. Are you happy?

BRIDEGROOM. Yes.

MOTHER. Where's your wife?

BRIDEGROOM. Having a bit of a rest. A bad day for brides!

MOTHER. A bad day? The only good one. For me it was like an inheritance.

The SERVANT *enters and goes towards the* BRIDE*'s room.*

The breaking-up of soil, the planting of new trees!

BRIDEGROOM. Are you thinking of going?

MOTHER. Yes. I must be at home.

BRIDEGROOM. You'll be alone.

MOTHER. No. My head's full of things and of men and fights.

BRIDEGROOM. But fights that aren't fights any more.

The SERVANT *enters quickly; she runs off via the backstage area.*

MOTHER. As long as you live, you struggle.

BRIDEGROOM. I'll always do what you tell me.

MOTHER. Try to be loving towards your wife, and if you find her uppity or stand-offish, give her a hug that hurts her a bit, a strong embrace, a bite, and then a gentle kiss. Not to annoy her, just to make her feel that you are the man, the master, the one who gives the orders. That's what I learned from your father. And because you don't have him, I must be the one to teach you how to be strong.

BRIDEGROOM. I'll always do what you want me to.

FATHER (*entering*). Where's my daughter?

BRIDEGROOM. She's inside.

FIRST GIRL. Let's have the bride and groom – we are going to do the round dance.

FIRST YOUTH (*to the* BRIDEGROOM). You are going to lead.

FATHER (*entering*). She isn't there.

BRIDEGROOM. No?

FATHER. She must have gone up to the balcony.

BRIDEGROOM. I'll go and see! (*He goes out.*)

A lot of noise and guitars.

FIRST GIRL. They've started! (*She leaves.*)

BRIDEGROOM (*entering*). She's not there.

MOTHER (*uneasily*). No?

FATHER. Where can she be?

SERVANT (*entering*). The girl, where is she?

MOTHER (*sombrely*). We don't know.

The BRIDEGROOM *goes out. Three* GUESTS *enter.*

FATHER (*dramatically*). But isn't she at the dance?

SERVANT. She's not at the dance.

FATHER (*strongly*). There's a crowd of people there. Look!

SERVANT. I've looked already.

FATHER (*darkly*). Well, where is she?

BRIDEGROOM (*entering*). No sign of her. Nowhere.

MOTHER (*to the* FATHER). What is this? Where is your daughter?

LEONARDO'*s* WIFE *enters.*

WIFE. They've run away! They've run away! Her and Leonardo. On horseback! Arms around one another!

Like a flash of lightning!

FATHER. It's not true! Not my daughter!

MOTHER. Yes. Your daughter! A plant from a wicked mother, and him, him too, him! But now she's my son's wife.

BRIDEGROOM (*entering*). We'll go after them! Who's got a horse?

MOTHER. Who's got a horse? Now! Who's got a horse? I'll give him everything I have. My eyes. Even my tongue . . .

VOICE. I'll go!

MOTHER (*to her son*). Go! After them! (*He goes out with two young men.*) No. Don't go! Those people kill quickly and well . . . But yes! Go on! I'll follow.

FATHER. It can't be her. Perhaps she's thrown herself into the water-tank.

MOTHER. Only decent and clean girls throw themselves into the water. Not that one! But now she's my son's wife. Two sides. Now there are two sides here. (*They all enter.*) My family and yours. All of you must go. Shake the dust from your shoes. Let's go and help my son. (*The people split into two groups.*) He's got plenty of family: his cousins from the coast and all those from inland. Go out from here! Search all the roads. The hour of blood has come again. Two sides. You on yours, me on mine. After them! Get after them!

Curtain.

Act Three

Scene One

A forest. It is night. Great moist tree trunks. A gloomy atmosphere. Two violins can be heard. Three WOODCUTTERS *appear.*

FIRST WOODCUTTER. Have they found them?

SECOND WOODCUTTER. No. But they are looking for them everywhere.

THIRD WOODCUTTER. They'll find them soon.

SECOND WOODCUTTER. Shhh!

THIRD WOODCUTTER. What?

SECOND WOODCUTTER. They seem to be coming near on all the roads at once.

FIRST WOODCUTTER. When the moon rises they'll see them.

SECOND WOODCUTTER. They should leave them alone.

FIRST WOODCUTTER. The world's big. Everyone can live in it.

THIRD WOODCUTTER. You have to follow your instinct. They were right to run away.

FIRST WOODCUTTER. They were deceiving each other. In the end the blood was strongest.

THIRD WOODCUTTER. The blood!

FIRST WOODCUTTER. You have to follow the blood's path.

SECOND WOODCUTTER. But blood that sees the light, the earth drinks it.

FIRST WOODCUTTER. What of it? Better to be a bloodless

corpse than alive and your blood putrid.

THIRD WOODCUTTER. Be quiet.

FIRST WOODCUTTER. Why? Can you hear something?

THIRD WOODCUTTER. I can hear the crickets, the frogs, the night lying in wait.

FIRST WOODCUTTER. But no sound of the horse.

THIRD WOODCUTTER. No.

FIRST WOODCUTTER. Now he'll be loving her.

SECOND WOODCUTTER. Her body for him, his body for her.

THIRD WOODCUTTER. They'll find them and they'll kill them.

FIRST WOODCUTTER. But they'll have mixed their blood by then. They'll be like two empty pitchers, like two dry streams.

SECOND WOODCUTTER. There are lots of clouds. Maybe the moon won't come out.

THIRD WOODCUTTER. Moon or no moon, the bridegroom will find them. I saw him leave. Like a raging star. His face the colour of ash. He contained the fate of his family.

FIRST WOODCUTTER. His family of dead men in the middle of the street.

SECOND WOODCUTTER. Yes.

THIRD WOODCUTTER. Do you think they can break through the circle?

SECOND WOODCUTTER. It's hard. There are knives and shotguns for ten leagues around.

THIRD WOODCUTTER. He has a good horse.

SECOND WOODCUTTER. But he's got a woman with him.

FIRST WOODCUTTER. We are close now.

SECOND WOODCUTTER. A tree with forty branches. We'll soon have it cut.

THIRD WOODCUTTER. The moon's coming out now. Let's hurry.

To the left, a patch of light.

FIRST WOODCUTTER. Oh rising moon!
Moon on the great leaves
SECOND WOODCUTTER. Fill the blood with jasmine!
FIRST WOODCUTTER. Oh lonely moon!
Moon on the green leaves!
SECOND WOODCUTTER. Silver on the bride's face!
THIRD WOODCUTTER. Oh evil moon!
Leave for their love a shadowy branch . . .
FIRST WOODCUTTER. Oh sad moon!
Leave for their love a branch in shadow!

They leave. In the light stage-left the MOON *enters. The* MOON *is a young woodcutter with a white face. The stage takes on an intense blue light.*

MOON. Round swan on the river,
Eye of the cathedrals,
False dawn amongst the leaves
Am I; they shall not escape!
Who is hiding? Who is sobbing
In the thick brush of the valley?
The moon places a knife
Abandoned in the sky,
That is a leaden ambush
And longs to be the pain of blood.
Let me come in! I come frozen
From walls and windows!
Open up roofs and hearts
Where I can warm myself!
I am cold! My ashes
Of dreaming metal
Seek the crest of fire
Through mountains and through streets.
But the snow bears me
On its back of jasper,
And water drowns me

Cold and hard in pools.
And so tonight there'll be
Red blood to fill my cheeks,
And the rushes forming clusters
At the wide feet of the wind.
Let there be no shadow, no hidden corner
To which they can escape!
For I want to enter a breast
Where I can warm myself!
A heart for me!
Warm!, that will spill
Over the mountains of my breast;
Let me come in, oh, let me in!

(*To the branches.*) I don't want shadows. My rays
Must enter everywhere,
And let there be among dark trunks
A murmur of gleaming light,
So that tonight there'll be
Red blood to fill my cheeks,
And the rushes forming clusters
At the wide feet of the wind.
Who is hiding? Come out, I say!
No! They shan't get away!
For I shall make the horse shine
With fever bright as diamond.

The MOON *disappears amongst the tree trunks and the stage becomes dark. An old* BEGGAR WOMAN *appears completely covered in thin dark-green cloth. Her feet are bare. Her face can hardly be seen amongst the folds. She is Death.*

BEGGAR WOMAN. The moon goes, and they come near.
From here they shan't move. The river's murmur
Shall drown with the whisper of the trees
The torn flight of their screams.
It shall be here, and soon. I'm tired.

They're opening the coffins, and white linen
waits, spread on bedroom floors,
For the weight of bodies with torn throats.
No bird shall awaken, and the breeze,
Gathering their cries in her skirt,
Shall fly with them over black tree-tops
Or bury them in soft slime.

(*Impatient.*) That moon! That moon!

The MOON *appears. The intense blue light returns.*

MOON. Now they come near.
Some through the ravine, others by the river.
I shall light up the stones. What do you need?

BEGGAR WOMAN. Nothing.

MOON. The wind is starting to blow hard, and double-edged.

BEGGAR WOMAN.
Light up the waistcoat, open the buttons,
For then the knives will know their path.

MOON. But let them die slowly. And let the blood
Place between my fingers its soft whistle.
See how my ashen valleys are awakening
With longing for this fountain and its trembling rush.

BEGGAR WOMAN. We mustn't let them get beyond the stream. Quiet!

MOON. There they come! (*He leaves. The stage is dark.*)

BEGGAR WOMAN.
Quickly! Lots of light! Do you hear me?
They can't escape!

The BRIDEGROOM *and the* FIRST YOUTH *appear. The* BEGGAR WOMAN *sits and covers her face with her cloak.*

BRIDEGROOM. This way.

FIRST YOUTH. You won't find them.

BRIDEGROOM (*forcefully*). I will find them.

FIRST YOUTH. I think they've gone by some other route.

BRIDEGROOM. No. I heard the sound of galloping a moment ago.

FIRST YOUTH. It must have been another horse.

BRIDEGROOM (*intensely*). Listen. There's only one horse in the whole world, and it's this one. Understand? If you come with me, come with me, but don't talk.

FIRST YOUTH. I wanted to . . .

BRIDEGROOM. Be quiet. I'm certain I'll find them here. You see this arm? Well it's not my arm. It's my brother's arm and my father's and my whole dead family's. And it's got such strength, it could tear this tree from its roots if it wanted to. Let's go quickly. I can feel the teeth of all my loved ones piercing me here so I can't breathe.

BEGGAR WOMAN (*moaning*). Oh!

FIRST YOUTH. Did you hear that?

BRIDEGROOM. Go that way and circle around.

FIRST YOUTH. This is a hunt.

BRIDEGROOM. A hunt. The greatest hunt of all.

The FIRST YOUTH *goes. The* BRIDEGROOM *moves quickly stage-left and stumbles over the* BEGGAR WOMAN.

BEGGAR WOMAN. Oh!

BRIDEGROOM. What do you want?

BEGGAR WOMAN. I'm cold.

BRIDEGROOM. Where are you going?

BEGGAR WOMAN (*always pleading like a beggar*). There . . . it's a long way.

BRIDEGROOM. Where have you come from?

BEGGAR WOMAN. There . . . it's a long way.

BRIDEGROOM. Did you see a man and a woman on horseback, galloping?

BEGGAR WOMAN (*awakening*). Wait . . . (*She looks at him.*) Such a good-looking boy if you were asleep!

BRIDEGROOM. Tell me. Answer. Did you see them?

BEGGAR WOMAN. Wait . . . Such broad shoulders! Why don't you like resting on them instead of walking on feet that are so small?

BRIDEGROOM (*shaking her*). I asked you if you saw them? Have they been this way?

BEGGAR WOMAN (*strongly*). No. They haven't. But they are coming from the hill. Can't you hear them?

BRIDEGROOM. No.

BEGGAR WOMAN. Don't you know the path?

BRIDEGROOM. I'll take it in any case.

BEGGAR WOMAN. I'll come with you. I know this land.

BRIDEGROOM (*impatient*). Let's go. Which way?

BEGGAR WOMAN (*strongly*). That way!

They leave quickly. In the distance two violins which represent the forest. The WOODCUTTERS *return. They carry axes on their shoulders. They move slowly amongst the tree trunks.*

FIRST WOODCUTTER. Oh rising death!
Death on the great leaves.

SECOND WOODCUTTER. Don't open the gush of blood!

FIRST WOODCUTTER. Oh, lonely death!
Death on the dry leaves!

THIRD WOODCUTTER. Don't cover the wedding with flowers!

SECOND WOODCUTTER. Oh sad death!
Leave for their love a green branch.

FIRST WOODCUTTER. Oh terrible death!
Leave for their love a green branch!

They exit as they are speaking. LEONARDO *and the* BRIDE *appear.*

LEONARDO. Quiet!

BRIDE. I'll go on my own from here.
You leave me! I want you to turn back.

LEONARDO. I said be quiet!

BRIDE. With your teeth,
With your hands, any way you can,
Tear the metal of this chain
From my pure throat,
And leave me locked away
Here in my house of earth.
And if you don't want to kill me
As you'd kill a tiny viper,
Put the barrel of your gun
In these bride's hands of mine.
Oh, what sorrow, what fire
Sweeps upward through my head!
What splinters of glass are stuck in my tongue!

LEONARDO. We've taken the step; quiet!
They are close behind us
And I'm taking you with me.

BRIDE. It will have to be by force!

LEONARDO. By force? Who was it went
Down the stairs first?

BRIDE. I did.

LEONARDO. Who was it put
A fresh bridle on the horse?

BRIDE. I did. It's true.

LEONARDO. Which hands
Strapped the spurs to my boots?

BRIDE. These hands, that are yours,
That when they see you want
To break the blue branches
And the whisper of your veins.
I love you! I love you! Leave me!
For if I could kill you,
I'd place a shroud over you
Edged with violet.
Oh, what sorrow, what fire
Sweeps upward through my head!

LEONARDO.
What splinters of glass are stuck in my tongue!
Because I wanted to forget
And I put a wall of stone
Between your house and mine.
It's the truth. Don't you remember?
And when I saw you from far away
I threw sand in my eyes.
But I'd get on the horse
And the horse would go to your door.
And then the silver wedding-pins
Turned my red blood black,
And our dream began to fill
My flesh with poisonous weeds.
Oh, I'm not the one at fault.
The fault belongs to the earth
And that scent that comes
From your breasts and your hair.

BRIDE. Oh, there's no reason! I don't want
Your blood or your table,
And there's not a minute of the day
That I don't want to be with you,
Because you drag me and I come,
And you tell me to go back
And I follow you through the air
Like a blade of grass.
I've left a good man
And all his family
In the middle of my wedding,
And wearing my bride's crown.
The punishment will fall on you,
And I don't want it to happen.
Leave me here! You go!
No one will defend you.

LEONARDO. Birds of early morning
Are waking in the trees.
The night is slowly dying
On the sharp edge of the stone.
Let's go to a dark corner
Where I can always love you
For to me people don't matter,
Nor the poison they pour on us.

He embraces her strongly.

BRIDE. And I will sleep at your feet
And watch over your dreams.
Naked, looking at the fields,
(*Powerfully.*) As if I were a bitch.
Because that's what I am! Oh, I look at you
And your beauty burns me.
LEONARDO. Flame is fired by flame.
And the same small flame
Can kill two ears of grain together.
Come on!

He pulls her.

BRIDE. Where are you taking me?
LEONARDO. To a place where they can't go,
These men who are all around us.
Where I can look at you!
BRIDE (*sarcastically*). Take me from fair to fair,
An insult to decent women,
So that people can see me
With my wedding sheets displayed
On the breeze, like banners.
LEONARDO. I want to leave you too,
If I thought as I ought to think.
But I go where you go.
And you too. Take a step. See.

Nails of moonlight join us,
My waist and your hips.

The whole scene is very strong, full of a great sensuality.

BRIDE. Listen!
LEONARDO. Someone's coming.
BRIDE. Go quickly!
It's right that I should die here,
My feet deep in the water
And thorns stuck in my head.
And let the leaves weep for me,
A woman lost and virgin.
LEONARDO. Be quiet! They are coming up.
BRIDE. Go!
LEONARDO. Quiet! Don't let them hear us.
You go first! Come on! Listen!

The BRIDE *hesitates.*

BRIDE. Both of us!
LEONARDO (*embracing her*). Whatever you want!
If they separate us, it will be
Because I am dead.
BRIDE. I will be dead too.

They leave embracing each other.

The MOON *appears slowly. The stage takes on a strong blue light. The two violins are heard. Suddenly two long, piercing screams and the music of the violins stops. With the second scream the* BEGGAR WOMAN *appears and stands with her back to the audience. She opens her cloak and stands centre-stage like a great bird with huge wings. The* MOON *stops. The curtain comes down in total silence.*

Scene Two

A white room with arches and thick walls. To the right and left white stairs. At the back a great arch and a wall of the same colour. The floor must also be a dazzling white. This simple room should have the monumental quality of a church. There must not be any grey, or shadow, anything that creates perspective.

Two GIRLS *dressed in dark blue are winding a skein of red wool.*

FIRST GIRL. Oh, wool, oh wool,
What will you make?

SECOND GIRL. A dress soft as jasmine,
Cloth paper-thin.
Begin it at four.
At ten finishing.
A thread of my wool's
A chain for your feet.
A knot that chokes,
The bride's bitter wreath.

LITTLE GIRL (*singing*). Did you see the wedding?

FIRST GIRL. No.

LITTLE GIRL I couldn't go!
What can have happened
Where the vine-shoots grow?
What can have happened
In the olive grove now?
What has happened?
No one's come home
Did you see the wedding?

SECOND GIRL. We've told you: no.

LITTLE GIRL (*leaving*). And I couldn't go!

SECOND GIRL. Oh wool, oh wool,
Of what will you sing?

FIRST GIRL. Of wounds like wax,
And myrtle's ache.
Of day's long sleep
And nights awake.

LITTLE GIRL (*at the door*).
The wool's caught
On a stone like a knife.
The blue mountains
Give it new life.
It runs, runs, runs,
By destiny led,
To cut with a knife
And take away bread.

She leaves.

SECOND GIRL. Oh wool, oh wool,
What will you say?
FIRST GIRL. The lover's dumb,
The young man red.
On the silent shore
I saw them spread.

She stops and gazes at the wool.

LITTLE GIRL (*appearing at the door*). Run, run, run.
Bring the wool here.
Covered in mud
I feel them come near.
Their bodies stiff
And the sheets marble-clear.

She leaves. Leonardo's WIFE *and* MOTHER-IN-LAW *appear.*

FIRST GIRL. Are they coming?
MOTHER-IN-LAW (*harshly*). We don't know.
SECOND GIRL. What can you tell us about the wedding?
FIRST GIRL. Tell me.
MOTHER-IN-LAW (*curtly*). Nothing.
WIFE. I want to go back to know all of it.
MOTHER-IN-LAW (*strongly*). You, to your house.
Brave and alone in your house.
To grow old and weep.

But the door always shut.
Never a soul. Dead or alive.
We'll nail up the windows.
And let the rains and the nights
Fall on the bitter weeds.

WIFE. What could have happened?

MOTHER-IN-LAW. It doesn't matter.
Cover your face with a veil.
Your children are your children,
There is nothing else. Over your bed
Place a cross of ash
Where once his pillow was.

They leave.

BEGGAR WOMAN (*at the door*). A piece of bread, little girls.

LITTLE GIRL. Go away!

The GIRLS *huddle together.*

BEGGAR WOMAN. Why?

LITTLE GIRL. Because you whine. Go away!

FIRST GIRL. Child!

BEGGAR WOMAN.
I could have asked for your eyes. A cloud
Of birds is following me. Would you like one?

LITTLE GIRL. I want to go home!

SECOND GIRL (*to the* BEGGAR WOMAN). Pay no attention!

FIRST GIRL. Did you come by the path along the stream?

BEGGAR WOMAN. I did.

FIRST GIRL (*timidly*). Can I ask you something?

BEGGAR WOMAN.
I saw them; they'll be here soon: two rushing streams
Still at last amongst the great stones,
Two men at the horse's feet,

Dead in the beauty of the night.
(*With pleasure.*)Dead, yes, dead!

FIRST GIRL. Be quiet, old woman, be quiet!

BEGGAR WOMAN.

Their eyes broken flowers, and their teeth
Two fistfuls of frozen snow.
Both of them fell, and the bride comes back,
Her skirt and her hair stained with their blood,
Covered by blankets both of them come,
Borne on the shoulders of tall young men.
That's how it was; no more, no less. Fitting.
Over the golden flower, dirty sand.

She goes. The GIRLS *incline their heads and begin to leave rhythmically.*

FIRST GIRL. Dirty sand.

SECOND GIRL. Over the golden flower.

LITTLE GIRL. Over the golden flower.
They are bringing the dead from the stream.
Dark-skinned the one,
Dark-skinned the other.
Oh, a nightingale's shadow flies and weeps
Over the golden flower!

She leaves. The stage is empty. The MOTHER *appears with a* NEIGHBOUR. *The* NEIGHBOUR *is weeping.*

MOTHER. Be quiet.

NEIGHBOUR. I can't.

MOTHER. I said be quiet. (*At the door.*) Is anyone there? (*She puts her hands to her forehead.*) My son should have answered. But my son's an armful of withered flowers now. My son's a fading voice beyond the mountains. (*Angrily, to the* NEIGHBOUR.) Won't you be quiet? I don't want weeping in this house. Your tears are tears that come from your eyes, that's all. But mine will come, when I'm all alone, from the soles of my feet, from my roots, and they'll burn hotter than blood.

NEIGHBOUR. Come to my house. Don't stay here.

MOTHER. Here. Here's where I want to be. At peace. All of them are dead now. At midnight I'll sleep, I'll sleep and not be afraid of a gun or a knife. Other mothers will go to their windows, lashed by the rain, to see the face of their sons. Not me. From my dream I'll fashion a dove of cold marble that will bear camellias of frost to the graveyard. But no, it's not a graveyard, not a graveyard: a bed of earth, a bed that shelters them and rocks them to sleep in the sky.

A WOMAN *enters, dressed in black. She goes to the right and kneels.*

(*To the* NEIGHBOUR.) Take your hands from your face. We have to face terrible days. I want to see no one. The earth and me. My grief and me. And these four walls. Oh! Oh!

She sits, overcome.

NEIGHBOUR. Have pity on yourself.

MOTHER (*smoothing her hair back*). I have to be calm. (*She sits.*) Because the neighbours will come and I don't want them to see me so poor. So poor! A woman without a single son she can hold to her lips.

The BRIDE *enters. She comes without the orange-blossom and wearing a black shawl.*

NEIGHBOUR (*angrily, seeing the* BRIDE). Where are you going?

BRIDE. I'm coming here.

MOTHER (*to the* NEIGHBOUR). Who is it?

NEIGHBOUR. Don't you know her?

MOTHER. That's why I'm asking who she is. Because I mustn't know her, so I shan't sink my teeth into her neck. Serpent!

She moves towards the BRIDE *threateningly; she stops.*

(*To the* NEIGHBOUR.) You see her? There, weeping, and me calm, without tearing her eyes out. I don't understand myself. Is it because I didn't love my son? But what about his name? Where is his name?

She strikes the BRIDE *who falls to the ground.*

NEIGHBOUR. In the name of God! (*She tries to separate them.*)

BRIDE (*to the* NEIGHBOUR). Leave her. I came so that she could kill me, so that they could bear me away with them. (*To the* MOTHER.) But not with their hands; with iron hooks, with a sickle, and with a force that will break it on my bones. Leave her! I want her to know that I'm clean, that even though I'm mad they can bury me and not a single man will have looked at himself in the whiteness of my breasts.

MOTHER. Be quiet, be quiet! What does that matter to me?

BRIDE. Because I went off with the other one! I went! (*In anguish.*) You would have gone too. I was a woman burning, full of pain inside and out, and your son was a tiny drop of water that I hoped would give me children, land, health; but the other one was a dark river, full of branches, that brought to me the sound of its reeds and its soft song. And I was going with your son, who was like a child of cold water, and the other one sent hundreds of birds that blocked my path and left frost on the wounds of this poor, withered woman, this girl caressed by fire. I didn't want to, listen to me! I didn't want to! Your son was my ambition and I haven't deceived him, but the other one's arm dragged me like a wave from the sea, like the butt of a mule, and would always have dragged me, always, always, even if I'd been an old woman and all the sons of your son had tried to hold me down by my hair!

A NEIGHBOUR *enters.*

MOTHER. She's not to blame! Nor me! (*Sarcastically.*) So who's to blame? A weak, delicate, restless woman who throws away a crown of orange-blossom to look for a piece of bed warmed by another woman!

BRIDE. Be quiet, be quiet! Take your revenge on me! Here I am! See how soft my throat is; less effort for you than cutting a dahlia in your garden. But no, not that! I'm pure, as pure as a new-born child. And strong enough to prove it to you. Light the fire. We'll put our hands in it: you for your son; me for my body. You'll be the first to take them out.

Another NEIGHBOUR *enters.*

MOTHER. What does your honour matter to me? What does your death matter to me? What does anything matter to me? Blessed be the wheat, for my sons lie beneath it. Blessed be the rain, for it washes the faces of the dead. Blessed be God, for He lays us side by side so we can rest.

Another NEIGHBOUR *enters.*

BRIDE. Let me weep with you.

MOTHER. Weep. But by the door.

The LITTLE GIRL *enters. The* BRIDE *remains by the door. The* MOTHER, *centre-stage.*

WIFE (*entering, moving stage-left*).
He was a handsome horseman,
Now a frozen heap of snow.
He rode to fairs and mountains
And the arms of women.
Now the dark moss of night
Forms a crown upon his brow.

MOTHER. Sunflower for your mother,
Mirror of the earth.

Let them place on your breast
A cross of bitter oleander;
A sheet to cover you
Of shining silk,
And let the water form its weeping
Between your still hands.

WIFE. Oh, four young men
Come with tired shoulders!

BRIDE. Oh, four handsome boys
Bear death on high.

MOTHER. Neighbours.

LITTLE GIRL (*at the door*). They are bringing them now.

MOTHER. It's the same.
The cross, the cross.

WOMEN. Sweet nails,
Sweet cross,
Sweet name
of Jesus.

BRIDE. Let the cross protect the living and the dead.

MOTHER. Neighbours: with a knife,
With a small knife,
On a day appointed, between two and three,
The two men killed each other for love.
With a knife,
With a small knife
That barely fits the hand,
But that slides in clean
Through startled flesh
And stops at the place
Where trembles, enmeshed,
The dark root of a scream.

BRIDE. And this is a knife,
A small knife
That barely fits the hand;
Fish without scales or river,

So that on a day appointed, between two and three,
With this knife
Two men are left stiff
And lips turned yellow.

MOTHER. That barely fits the hand,
But that slides in clean
Through startled flesh
And stops there, at the place
Where trembles enmeshed
The dark root of a scream.

The neighbours are kneeling and weeping.

Curtain.

Notes

Act One

Scene One

3 *Room painted yellow*: Lorca's initial stage direction is as terse as the dialogue that follows it. The yellow of the walls has been seen by some critics as relating to wheat, virility and thus the Bridegroom. See, for example, Robert Barnes, 'The Fusion of Poetry and Drama in *Blood Wedding*'. This may be so and is certainly reinforced by many subsequent images in the play, as in the case of the Mother's words later in this scene: 'That's what I like. Men to be men; wheat wheat.' But Lorca's images frequently suggest the co-existence or proximity of opposites – the lemon is bright but bitter, and the Mother's 'golden boy' will become by the time the action of the play is over a corpse that is 'left stiff / And lips turned yellow'. The initial setting, therefore, is already two things in one: the Mother's hope and fear, the Bridegroom's youthful and optimistic present touched by darker hints of what the future holds.

the knife: the allusion to the knife provides a good example of the way in which in Lorca's work a prosaic, concrete object, often connected with rural life, is the starting-point from which a whole range of much more general resonances and associations open out. For the Bridegroom the knife is meaningful here only as an instrument for cutting grapes; for the Mother it is the means whereby the lives of her husband and her other son were cut short, in other words a reminder of that fatality that hangs like the sword of Damocles over the characters of this play and whose cutting-edge is glimpsed throughout it, be it in the glint in the horse's eyes ('A silver dagger broken', Act One, Scene Two), the axes of the Woodcutters (Act Three, Scene One), or the knife that in the song of the three girls cuts the wool (Act

Three, Scene Two), that is to say, the thread of life. Through the ordinary, everyday, visible objects of the characters' experience we are made aware in the most telling way of the unseen forces that are an equally real part of their world.

4 *to put a palm-leaf on him or a plateful of coarse salt*: the association of the palm-leaf with death and the placing of weight on the stomach of a corpse to prevent swelling are both part of the traditions of Andalusia, in particular of rural people.

the scent of carnation: see p. xxxviii for Mildred Adams' comments on the New York production in 1934: 'They found the Mother's passionate way of addressing her beloved son as "my carnation" merely funny.' While it is the dead husband, not the son, who is referred to as 'carnation', Adams' point suggests the potential difficulty for a largely urban audience in approaching the work of a poet-dramatist whose imagery is so rooted in the countryside, and beyond that in a Spanish tradition in which such allusions are perfectly common. Just afterwards, for example, the Mother speaks of her late husband and her son as 'two men who were two geraniums', and in Act One, Scene Two, the Wife says of her child: 'He's like a dahlia today'. In translation the images cannot and should not be toned-down or avoided. Lorca's touch is always very sure in this respect, and the task of bringing out the full force of what is usually a beautiful and very effective comparison falls to the actor and the director of a given piece.

5 *the vineyards*: there are frequent allusions in Lorca's plays to the natural world as the setting for love-making, of the inter-relationship, therefore, of the activities of human beings and the land to which they are shown to be so close. In *The House of Bernarda Alba*, for example, the olive-grove is where a group of young men make love to the village-girl, Paca la Rosita. In *Yerma*, on the other hand, a powerful contrast is drawn between Juan's cultivation of his fields and his neglect of his wife, while for Yerma herself the spectacle of Nature's fertility is an agonising reminder of her own lack of a child.

You old woman . . .: this incident stems from Lorca's own habit of picking up his mother, who was quite small.

one of the Félixes could die, one of the family of murderers: the family feud which has led to the death of the Mother's husband

and elder son at the hands of the Félixes is never explained clearly, though we gather from her that the murderers are in jail and from the Neighbour later in the scene that the Bridegroom was 'eight years old when those things happened'. It seems quite likely, given the emphasis on land in the play, that the bitterness between the two families is one that has its roots in some argument over ownership, a common enough occurrence in rural communities.

6 *One woman with one man*: from the outset the Mother is shown to be the spokeswoman for extremely traditional attitudes, both moral and social, though we soon see that she is echoed in this respect by the father of the Bride and the mother-in-law of Leonardo. In short, traditional attitudes are voiced by the older people in the play, while the young people – particularly the Bride and Leonardo – embody natural instincts and passions which, given free rein, run counter to traditional values. It is a conflict which Lorca expresses in many plays – *The Shoemaker's Wonderful Wife, Yerma, The House of Bernarda Alba* – as well as in his poetry, and of which he, as a homosexual in a narrow-minded society, was only too painfully aware.

brass earrings: see p. 64, note on the colour yellow. Since the earrings are a present to the bride-to-be, the colour is here part of the play's more positive and optimistic thrust.

7 *The* MOTHER *remains seated*: the Mother's seated posture – and she remains seated for a considerable part of the ensuing dialogue with the Neighbour – is one which suggests very effectively her despondent mood. It is a visual image which Lorca used quite often throughout his plays, as in the seated, despairing figure of Mariana Pineda in the last act of the play of the same name, or the seated figures of the daughters in *The House of Bernarda Alba*, engaged in their monotonous task of sewing and resigned to their fate. But the position of the figure is, it should be noted, only part of the overall image, and in this first scene the Mother and the Neighbour are dressed in dark clothes against a background of yellow. The overall effect is inevitably stark and suggests, as do all Lorca's stage-pictures, the predominant mood of the scene, which is one of great foreboding.

7 *no chance of being crippled*: the misfortune of the Mother is echoed by that of the Neighbour, whose son is dead, and by that of another neighbour, whose son's arms have been 'cut clean off by the machine'. Through the linking of different families to misfortune – and the same is true of *The House of Bernarda Alba* – the sense is strongly conveyed of a fatality that is inevitable and cyclic, as irresistible as the cycle of Nature itself.

8 *the girl or her mother*: to translate the Spanish literally here would give a very awkward expression – 'I wish that no one knew them, either the one who's alive or the one who's dead.'

9 *such a hot day?*: a close parallel is established in this and other plays between the heat of the summer, which oppresses the characters externally, and the heat of passion which comes from within. A particularly powerful example occurs at the beginning of Act Two of *The House of Bernarda Alba* where the restlessness of the daughters at night may be attributed to the intolerable heat, but also in some cases to the sexual desire and frustration that boils within them. The double assault of climate and passion, both of which seem inescapable, heightens the feeling in Lorca's work of a fate that is inevitable.

she stops and slowly crosses herself: here, clearly, background, costume and movement combine to create a visual image of the Mother's despair. The interplay of yellow and black is far from comforting, communicating to the spectator of the scene the Mother's bitterness and sense of foreboding. Her slow movement too reinforces the sense of fear, even despair, that is burdensome, while the action of crossing herself is a gesture that tells us immediately that she not only hopes against hope but believes that the future is not in her own hands. The importance of the sets in the overall effect means, of course, that a performance 'in the round' cannot be wholly satisfactory.

Scene Two

9 *A room painted pink*: the setting is a marked contrast to that which opens Scene One. Here there is at first no harshness; rather the pink of the walls, the glow of burnished copper, the bright colours of flowers, and the light of morning, all of which create a mood that is both tranquil and optimistic. In addition,

the position of the two women, seated opposite each other, one knitting, the other rocking the child to sleep, reinforces the overall sense of balance, harmony and tranquillity. And this is enhanced by the initial soothing tones of the lullaby. Again it is clear that the effect would be somewhat lost by a performance 'in the round'.

Lullaby, my baby sweet: in 1928 Lorca gave a lecture on lullabies. See *Deep Song and Other Prose*, ed. and trans. by Christopher Maurer. He alluded there to six versions of the traditional lullaby, the most popular in the province of Granada, which he reworked in his play, and, in the course of commenting on it, drew particular attention to the way in which (a) Spain uses its saddest songs and its most melancholy texts to touch the first sleep of her children, and (b) the child sees neither the horse nor the rider of the lullaby face to face but only glimpses them in the half-light and is made to feel the intense anguish of that moment.

10 *For the horse will not drink deep*: Lorca transforms the traditional lullaby, where the rider does not allow the horse to drink, into something altogether more menacing, for it is now the horse's instinct which tells it not to drink from the deep, black and anguished water.

my little rose: the allusion to the child in terms which evoke its delicacy and beauty sets it firmly in the context of the bright and optimistic colouring of the room, but already this is offset by the lullaby's evocation of the dark water and the fearful horse that 'now starts to weep'.

A silver dagger broken: the reflection of the water in the horse's eyes glints like silver or steel. Through the image of a dagger a link is established with the knife of Scene One, which has led already to two deaths, and the knives that finally end the lives of the Bridegroom and Leonardo. The horse of the lullaby, moreover, anticipates the horse of Leonardo himself which, as the result of his death, will be left without a rider, just as the child will be left without a father. Again, the horse's bleeding legs suggest the human blood that has been and will be shed, and this in turn places the innocent child in the context of an adult world which is full of violence.

his mouth is hot: the heat and the thirst of the horse parallel Leonardo's passionate desire for the Bride, while the dry river bed, a few lines later, is a pointer to his subsequent death, when the vital flow of life is suddenly stilled.

11 *Close the window*: the closed window is here associated with the warmth and safety of the sleeping child. Later in the play it becomes a metaphor for the anguish of widows – the Bride and the wife of Leonardo – who will be obliged to 'grow old and weep' behind closed doors and windows. See Act Three, Scene Two.

a nice soft pillow: the child, comforted by its mother and comfortable too in its soft, warm bed, becomes later on the dead man whose bed is the earth and whose pillow is 'a cross of ash'. See Act Three, Scene Two.

the mare will waiting be: the lines of the lullaby both anticipate the Bride's suppressed longing for Leonardo and emphasise once more the force of instinct and passion in the lives of the characters. For a more detailed and extremely perceptive analysis of the lullaby, see *Bodas de sangre*, ed. H. Ramsden, pp.76–8.

He's like a dahlia today: see p. 65, note on 'the scent of carnation'.

12 *the other side of the plains*: the play has a great sense of space which contributes to its universality. Leonardo, as this example suggests, travels far on the horse. The 'dry place', where he has been seen, is said later to be four hours' journey from where the Mother and the Bridegroom live (Act One, Scene Three) and therefore far too from Leonardo's home. Later, for the wedding in Act Two, the guests come from far away, some of the Mother's relatives from the coast, and at the end of the act the Bride and Leonardo escape on horseback and ride off into the great forest, the setting for Act Three. The geography of the play, ranging as it does, is never precise, but it is, of course, the lack of precision, like the names of the characters, which transforms the action into something much more symbolic. The dry, hot lands where the Bride lives and burns with suppressed longing draw the fiery Leonardo to them and they become, appropriately, the dominant, central landscape of the play. It is appropriate too that the lovers, responding to natural instinct,

should take refuge in the great, damp, fertile forest. But the geography of the play works in another way too, for by the final act the action has moved away from the particular and the temporal into a timeless world inhabited by Death and the Fates, and also, it can be argued, particularly in Act Three, Scene One, into the inner world of the lovers' guilt and fear, exteriorised in the fearful shadows and apparitions of the forest. There is a useful study of this aspect of the play by C. B. Morris, *García Lorca: Bodas de sangre*, Critical Guides to Spanish Texts, in particular pp. 58–67.

With the water really cold: just before this Leonardo's horse has been described as 'half-dead from sweating'. His own thirst here parallels that of the horse, linking the instincts of beast and man, though Leonardo's thirst is also of another kind and will not be alleviated by a drink of lemon. Indeed, the lemon is a reminder to us that all is not well in Leonardo's household and immediately precedes his bitter quarrel with his mother-in-law and then his wife.

as if he's come from the end of the world: a good example of the way in which a comment by one of the characters 'opens up' the play symbolically and poetically. As far as the horse is concerned, it can, like other images and symbols in the play, be seen in different and often contrasting ways: firstly, as an image of unfettered male vitality; but secondly, and in particular through the implications of the lullaby, as the instrument of fate which bears Leonardo to the Bride and ultimately to his death. The association of horse and fate is to be found in much of Lorca's work, as in the 'Dialogue of Amargo, the Bitter One', in Lorca's volume of poetry, *Poem of Deep Song*, where on the road to Granada a young man meets a mysterious rider whose brothers sell knives. The dark horse and its enigmatic rider are, of course, Death, and the piece ends with the young man's scream as the rider insists that he take a knife.

14 *Two fortunes joined together*: considerable emphasis is given to money and land as a prime motivation in the marriage of the Bride and the Bridegroom. Lorca is, of course, criticising a marriage that is arranged for the wrong reasons and a society that continues to give its support to such a tradition. In *Blood Wedding* the consequences of the marriage are tragic. In earlier

plays, such as *The Shoemaker's Wonderful Wife*, the matter is presented in a much more comic, even farcical way, but even there the underlying sadness of the ill-matched couple is very evident.

LEONARDO *leaves*: if this scene begins quietly, it becomes progressively more agitated, and this is expressed both in the sharp, rapier-like exchanges between the three characters and in the movements of Leonardo in particular as he enters, turns on the young girl, sits, gets up and storms out. It is another example of Lorca's integration of setting, lighting, movement and speech, as powerful as that of Scene One but quite different in its impact.

15 *now starts to weep*: the conclusion of the scene links the weeping of the horse in the lullaby to the weeping of the women themselves, and thus the horse's irrational fear to their sense of foreboding in relation to what lies ahead. And this, of course, echoes the Mother's fears as she crosses herself at the end of Scene One. The whole of Scene Two is seen to be, in effect, a disturbing but remorseless stripping-away of the optimism which colours its beginning, and its ending, though paralleling the opening in some ways, is really quite different in its effect. It is worth noting too that in terms of age the characters in it range from infancy to young adulthood and, in the case of the Mother-in-Law, widowhood: in short, the span of human life, and all of it touched by suffering.

Scene Three

15 *Interior of the cave . . .*: in its predominant colours, especially pink, the setting echoes the beginning of Scene Two. To that extent the house of the Bride, and therefore the Bride herself, is linked to the house of Leonardo, and by the same token is separated from the house of the Bridegroom in Scene One. Each time the curtain rises, or the stage lights go up, the stage picture is an instant reminder of the key relationships in the play, as well as creating in the audience an initial sense of the mood of a scene which may, of course, be sustained or dispelled in the course of it. In addition, whiteness points to the purity and innocence of the Bride, though given the fact that in Lorca

colours often suggest more than one thing, it also anticipates the Bridegroom's shroud, the coldness of death and the subsequent emptiness of the Bride's life.

16 *a chain of gold*: see p. 64, note on the colour yellow. While the Mother's black dress and the Bridegroom's black suit indicate that their visit is a formal one, the colour is also ominous, recalling the dark clothes of the women in Scene One, and in the sense that it is set here against the white walls it already points to the fact that hope and innocence are already threatened.

seated, stiff as statues: posture and movement combine with costume to suggest the formality of the occasion and thus the importance of tradition in the lives of these characters.

shining white hair: the predominant whiteness of the room itself is maintained, though in this case it has the effect of presenting the Father as a patriarchal figure. The Father's age is not given, but if, as we are told, his daughter is only twenty-one, he is unlikely to be as old as the stage direction suggests. There are several instances in the play where Lorca loses sight of the probability of things in the interests of a greater dramatic or symbolic effect. On these inconsistencies, see *Bodas de sangre*, ed. H. Ramsden, pp. xlv–xlix.

Four hours: see p. 69, note, 'the other side of the plains'.

17 *even make it suffer*: the Father speaks of his fields as if they were human, again establishing that relationship between Man and Nature that is such a distinctive feature of the play.

worth a fortune: see p. 70, note, 'Two fortunes joined together'. While Lorca is undoubtedly critical of a situation in which land and property take precedence over love, it has to be understood that in rural communities the ownership of land is synonymous with achievement, gives identity and assures continuity. It is not so much a case, therefore, of consciously putting these things first as of behaving in a way which is deeply ingrained.

They've talked it over: the fact that the Bride and the Bridegroom have talked things over seems to suggest that they are not being pushed into it. On the other hand, there can be no doubt that the Bride's father and the Bridegroom's mother both see the marriage as a convenient one and make every effort to bring it about. And even if the Bride is in agreement, it is soon made very clear that her feelings for the Bridegroom are far less strong than his for her. Her motives, as we see later, involve a strong element of pride and spite towards Leonardo which are far greater than her love for the Bridegroom – in short, a betrayal of her instincts.

18 *She's breaking up bread at three*: a reference to a traditional practice of breaking bread into crumbs, soaking it in water and salt and frying it in olive oil. The men of the family would eat this dish for breakfast before going to work in the fields.

Next Thursday: this short space of time would hardly allow the banns to be read and all the necessary arrangements made. Many of the wedding guests – see p. 69, note, 'the other side of the plains' – come from far away and there would clearly be insufficient time to invite them. Furthermore, in Scene Two, Leonardo's wife has observed that the wedding will take place 'in less than a month', which presumably means at least three weeks. It seems strange that these inconsistencies should not have been cleared up, but there can be no doubt that the compression of the action into a shorter period of time makes it much more urgent and dramatic, and this, clearly, was uppermost in Lorca's mind.

19 *She's like my wife in every way*: in Scene One the Neighbour has observed of the Bride's mother: 'She didn't love her husband.' The eagerness of the Bridegroom's mother to know all she can about the Bride's background stems from her conviction that sons follow their fathers and girls their mothers: a characteristic of Lorca's Andalusian world in which the notion of heredity is very strong, reinforcing the notion of destiny and fatality. Thus, the Bride, though basically good, will not love her husband – at least, not strongly enough – and the Bridegroom's death, at the hands of the Félix family, parallels his father's.

a kind of lump in my throat: there are movements like this when the Bridegroom strikes us as naive, awkward and sexually inexperienced. His mother has stated earlier in the scene that 'He's never known a woman', and here, we note, he refuses a drink in favour of a sweetmeat. Indeed, he seems to be rather insipid throughout Acts One and Two and only becomes a strong character and a worthy opponent for Leonardo in Act

Three when, in pursuit of the escaping lovers, the passion and strength of his whole family drives him on as though he were only an instrument with which to extract their vengeance.

20 *I wish I was one*: clearly a cry of protest against the subservience of women, so often obliged in this society to obey their parents' wishes in relation to marriage. It is echoed in *Yerma*, Act One, Scene Two, by the Second Girl: 'If we go on like this, the only girls not married will be the little ones . . . I'm nineteen, and I can't stand cooking and washing. The whole day I've got to be doing the things I hate. And what for? Why has my husband got to be my husband?' The theme of conformity to the standards imposed by society runs through *The House of Bernarda Alba* too, and the position of women in relation to it is stated clearly by the old servant, La Poncia, in Act Two: '. . . and the girl who doesn't conform can cry in the corner and rot.'

The light begins to fade: in terms of the realism of the play there is an inconsistency here, for if, as we have been told earlier in the scene, the Mother and the Bridegroom have a four-hour journey in front of them, it is unlikely that they would set out just as it is beginning to get dark. Clearly, what was more important to Lorca than accuracy or consistency was a dramatic ending to the act, which is achieved very strikingly here as the light fades and the Servant discloses the Bride's secret rendezvous with Leonardo. And, of course, the descent of night has a metaphorical significance too, for it points to the darkness of passion in which the Bride is about to be engulfed.

Act Two

Scene One

22 *in this heat*: the darkness of night, emphasised at the end of Act One, is now combined with its heat, and both suggest, of course, the inescapable and suffocating nature of the Bride's longing for Leonardo as her marriage to the Bridegroom draws near. There is a very similar situation at the beginning of Act Three of *The House of Bernarda Alba* where the women's description of the oppressive heat of the previous night is a

pointer to their sexual frustration. In the case of the Bride, the white of Act One, Scene Three, is echoed now in her petticoat and continues to suggest virginity.

Her fate: see p. 73, note, 'She's like my wife . . .' Once more the parallel between mother and daughter is emphasised.

23 *Or plenty of bitterness*: the orange-blossom, which the Servant is about to fix in the Bride's hair, is traditionally associated with marriage, but the orange, both in traditional Spanish poetry and in Lorca's poetry and drama, is synonymous with sweetness, in contrast to the lemon and the grapefruit, both of which represent bitterness. In the exchanges here a striking contrast is developed in the nature of the dialogue itself, for the Servant's description of love and marriage, erotic and sensual, is at every step countered by the Bride's curt and impatient rejoinders.

24 *Oh let the bride awaken now*: the lullaby of Act One, Scene Two, is, as we have seen, based on a traditional lullaby, though Lorca reworked it for his own purposes. The wedding-song does not seem to be based on any particular song, though it reveals clearly enough the influence of traditional songs and ballads. Lorca reworked traditional material in his own way so that the imagery of the song is closely integrated into that of the play as a whole. Thus, the Servant's opening lines, with their references to flowing rivers and flowering laurel, initiates the theme and the mood of creativity, fertility and optimism that surround the marriage ceremony.

If he dies, he dies: again a parallel exists between the horse driven by Leonardo and the latter driven by his instincts and passions, and there is, of course, an unconscious irony in the sense that Leonardo's horse does not die, but he does.

25 *That's the thorn*: Leonardo's bitterness is occasioned in no small measure by the belief that the Bride has turned away from him – or been persuaded to turn away from him – on account of his poor circumstances, and a few lines further on he refers to the 'silver' for which she has now settled, an allusion no doubt to the betrayal of Christ by Judas. The reference to the thorn here – Leonardo's sense of injury at being abandoned for lack of land and wealth – may be linked to the Bride's father's use of the same word (Act One, Scene Three) to describe his regret at not owning a particular field. Thus the preoccupation of these

people with land and property and its central effect on their lives is again highlighted.

26 *I'm a man of honour*: the theme of honour is important in the play in a variety of ways. Leonardo is suggesting here that he is not the sort of man to spread rumours about the Bride which will lead people to gossip about her and therefore tarnish her public image or reputation. This concept of honour, with its emphasis on public opinion, runs through the theatre of Lorca, as it does, indeed, through Spanish literature of earlier centuries, in particular of the sixteenth and seventeenth centuries, where it manifested itself so strongly in such plays as Calderón's *The Surgeon of Honour* and *The Painter of Dishonour*. Leonardo's assertion that he is a man of integrity points too, however, to the idea of honour as virtue and moral uprightness, a rather different aspect of honour which is also central to Lorca's work. For a general study of the subject see J. Pitt-Rivers, 'Honour and Social Status', *Honour and Shame: The Values of Mediterranean Society*, ed. J. G. Peristiany (London, 1965), pp. 19–77.

insinuations about the orange-blossom: the orange-blossom is, of course, white and therefore a symbol of purity.

To keep quiet and burn: Leonardo's blazing passion is suggested by his name, for its second half 'ardo' means 'I burn', while the first half, 'León' (lion), points to the strength of his passion as well as to his animal energy in general. He is the only character in the play who is given a real name, but even so it is highly symbolic.

27 *my heart's putrified*: the effect of frustrated desire is revealed in many of Lorca's plays. When in *The House of Bernarda Alba*, Act Three, the unfortunate Martirio reveals her secret longing for the young man, Pepe el Romano, she describes the release of her contained emotion in terms of a pomegranate bursting. In a rather different sense Yerma's unfulfilled longing for a child slowly poisons her: 'All women have blood enough for four or five children, and when they are left with none, the blood turns sour, as mine must' (Act One, Scene One).

Let the bride awaken now: in contrast to the tense and bitter confrontation between the Bride and Leonardo, the arrival of the wedding guests transforms the mood of the scene into one of joy and optimism, emphasising the vital and creative significance of marriage. It is essential, of course, that in performance the speaking or chanting of these lines and the movements of the characters who deliver them be choreographed in a way which gives the scene its maximum impact. Lorca himself once observed: 'Seldom do we Andalusians notice the "middle tone". An Andalusian either shouts at the stars or kisses the red dust of the road' (see *Deep Song and Other Prose*, trans. C. Maurer, p. 32). In order to know how the poetry of Lorca's plays should be spoken, one need only see a good production by a Spanish company or listen to recorded readings of both the plays and the poetry. Part of the problem for English actors in performing Lorca's plays is, needless to say, their lack of familiarity with the Spanish tradition.

28 *flowering bough*: the joyous song is filled with images of growth and vitality – 'The flowering bough / Of laurel'; 'let flowers now / Your balconies array'; 'Head adorned by jasmine sweet'.
the olive grove: a frequent Lorca metaphor for fertility and growth. See p. 65, note, 'the vineyards'.
Trays of dahlias: another image of beauty and vitality, the dahlia having been used earlier in Act One, Scene Two, to describe Leonardo's child.
the grape-fruit tree: the Spanish word 'toronjil' means either grapefruit or orange-grove and is therefore, in terms of its double meaning, highly appropriate to the Bride's bitter-sweet anticipation of her marriage. Since it is impossible to translate the double-meaning in English, I have opted for 'grapefruit' on the grounds that the Servant, well aware of the Bride's feelings, would probably deliver the lines in an ironic tone which stresses their negative rather than positive meaning, even though the other guests will not be aware of that.

29 *Adorned with ribbons of darkest red*: the idea of the genealogical tree runs through the play and is used as well by Lorca to reinforce the relationship between human beings and the natural world. Here the 'ribbons of darkest red' are, of course, the branches of the tree which the Servant proposes to embroider, while red also brings to mind blood running

through veins – themselves a network of branches – and thus the vitality of human life and human relationships.

a golden flower: see p. 64, note, 'Room painted yellow'. The evocation of the Bridegroom's youth, looks and vitality here should be contrasted with the images of the play's final scene where yellow is synonymous with death: 'That's how it was; no more, no less. Fitting. / Over the golden flower, dirty sand.'

30 *Like a great bull*: again suggestive of vigour and vitality. We recall the Mother's description of her husband in Act One, Scene One: 'Is it possible that a thing as small as a pistol or a knife can put an end to a man who's a bull?'

She wears a black dress: apart from the fact that in Spanish rural communities' brides often wore a black wedding-dress, it has here both dramatic and symbolic force. On the one hand, it contrasts vividly with the colour and animation introduced by the arrival of the wedding guests. On the other, the visual contrast, arresting in itself, is a pointer to the Bride's inner feelings, in particular repressed passion which, turning in on itself, putrifies. See p. 76, note, 'my heart's putrified'. We are reminded too of the lullaby, Act One, Scene Two, and the black water which ominously stops at the bridge, while later, Act Three, Scene One, Leonardo describes his frustration as turning 'my red blood black'. Finally, black already looks forward to the moment when the Bride will become a widow and assume the traditional colour of mourning, worn by the Mother throughout the play.

31 *if my mother were to call me*: see p. 73, note, 'She's like my wife . . .'. The Bride's words now seem to suggest that not only did her mother not love her husband but that she was involved with another man and in spirit is encouraging the Bride to follow a similar course of action.

The sun has risen: in terms of the lighting of the stage, the scene is a progression from its initial suggestion of night to daybreak as the guests arrive – *It starts to get light* – and finally sunrise as they leave for the ceremony in the church. As the great door opens backstage, the stage will clearly be flooded with sunlight, an effect which encapsulates the optimism of the wedding guests and is emotionally uplifting in relation to the audience.

32 *A thorn in each eye*: see for example, p. 75, note, 'That's the thorn'. Like so many other images in the play, it illustrates very well Lorca's use of ordinary, concrete things to create effects that are immediate and palpable.

My mother's fate was the same: see p. 73, note, 'She's like my wife . . .'. The Wife's experience will echo her mother's as the Bride's will echo hers and the Mother's loss of her husband and elder son will be repeated in the Bridegroom's death at the hands of the same family. The theme of heredity and its implications is touched upon throughout the play.

Like a bright star shining: the wedding-song is in the Spanish text characterised not by rhyme but by assonance. In the English translation I have opted for a good deal of rhyme, since assonance is difficult to transpose into English and rhyme does, of course, provide the kind of spring that the song requires.

Scene Two

33 *a landscape in popular ceramic*: allusions in Lorca which at first seem obscure usually have a very simple explanation. The reference to ceramic means, as the earlier part of the stage direction suggests, that the setting has the hard outline, the cold feeling and the flat colours of a land which has been burnt by the sun of centuries. This is, after all, the 'dry lands', and Lorca's intention is once again to place before us, prior to the appearance of the characters, a landscape which is harsh and forbidding and which in that sense already encapsulates the mood of the ensuing action.

The wheel was turning: the Servant's song combines the optimistic implications of the wedding-song of the previous scene with the ominous overtones of the lullaby of Act One, Scene Two. In contrast to the water of the lullaby, which stops at the bridge, the water now flows freely, the branches part and the moon shines brightly. But if these allusions evoke the joy and celebration that are normally associated with marriage, the references to branches and moon anticipate too the forest of Act Three, Scene One, where the Bride hides with Leonardo, and the moon which illuminates the spot where Leonardo and the Bridegroom fight to the death.

Let the almond's bitterness / Be honey's sweetness: see p. 75, note, 'Or plenty of bitterness'. Again the Servant's song, like the whole of the wedding scene, voices a communal optimism with which the Bride's true feelings are, as we know, at variance.

34 *For fresh blood running*: an allusion to the penetration of the virgin on her wedding-night, and also to the children to whom her blood will be passed. But simultaneously we are reminded of the blood that runs when flesh is pierced by knives, of the Mother's anguished past on that account and her fears for the future. Lorca's ability to invest a word or image with different and often contradictory resonances is quite startling, constantly creating those tensions out of which drama is made.

The blood of his entire family: the Mother immediately transforms the optimistic allusions to blood in the Servant's song into something much more pessimistic. On the theme of the family-tree see p. 77, note, 'Adorned with ribbons of darkest red'. See too Eva K. Touster, 'Thematic Patterns in Lorca's *Blood Wedding*', *Modern Drama*, 7.

35 *hide it in these shawls*: there is a clear parallel between the Mother, driven mad by the fact of having to stifle and contain her grief and rage, and the Bride, her heart putrified by repressed passion. The links between individuals in terms of their suffering emerge slowly in the first three scenes of the play where the Mother's anguish (Scene One) becomes the Wife's (Scene Two) and then the Bride's (Scene Three). The process is one which is extended, as the action unfolds, to embrace individuals and families in an ever-widening circle of suffering. By its conclusion the Mother and the Bride are, of course, united in their grief and their widow's weeds.

My son will cover her well: again human sexual union is described, quite naturally by the Mother, in terms of the mating of animals, in particular horses and bulls. And when, in the very next phrase, she alludes to her son as 'of good seed', there is an immediate association in her mind and ours between the sperm that makes the woman fertile and the seed that germinates in good soil.

A fountain that spurts for a minute: this image contains many resonances. On the one hand, the use of the word 'fountain' conjures up a picture of water and therefore growth and vitality. It links too with the allusion to sexual union made in the Mother's previous speech and evokes the sperm that spurts for a moment. On the other hand, unlike water, blood that falls on the ground is useless, wasted, unproductive, a sense of waste that is very powerfully suggested by the Mother's attempt to recover her son's blood before the earth soaks it up.

36 *Whole branches of families*: see p. 77, note, 'Adorned with ribbons . . .'. It is important too to bear in mind the role of the Woodcutters in Act Three, Scene One, and the knives that will eventually fell not branches of trees but two young men, the vigorous growth of two different families.

as light as a dove: Lorca's gift for choosing the right image is almost unerring. The allusion to the dove immediately opens up in our mind's eye a sense of space, soaring and freedom and thus of the uplifting nature of marriage with its perspectives of hope and happiness. And the force of that image is, of course, intensified by the reality, on stage before us, of the Bride not uplifted but already burdened by and confined by a marriage she does not really want.

37 *We've got no money*: the Wife's complaint about their poor financial circumstances reinforces the impression that the relative wealth of the Bride's father and the Bridegroom's mother is certainly an important factor in the marriage of their children. See p. 75, note, 'That's the thorn'.

38 *a lively interplay of figures*: the scene as a whole, in terms both of movement and of dialogue, is constructed with considerable theatrical skill. As far as movement is concerned, from the moment the guests enter, there is a constant shift of focus from individual to individual and group to group: the Father, the Mother, the Bride, the Bridegroom; the Wife and the Bridegroom; the Servant and the Bridegroom; the Bride and the two girls, etc. But this kaleidoscope of movement, which suggests so well the bustle and activity of a wedding reception, is more importantly an interweaving of individual and collective tensions which are revealed, as it were, in snatches but which, taken together, build remorselessly to the climax of the scene.

Lively old women: Lorca's Servant, like many of the older servants in his plays, is based not only on the old women with whom he came into contact in Granada and the surrounding area but the servants in his own family who cared for him as a child. Foremost amongst these was Dolores la Colorina, who taught Lorca many of the traditional poems, songs and lullabies to be found in his work and of which the lullaby of *Blood Wedding*, Act One, Scene Two, is a fine example. In the plays as a whole there are many finely-drawn old servants, the best two arguably being La Poncia in *The House of Bernarda Alba* and the housekeeper in *Doña Rosita the Spinster*, both of them distinguished by their practical commonsense and earthy humour.

I don't eat in the middle of the night: in discussing Lorca's theatre, and particularly plays like the three so-called rural tragedies, it is important not to neglect those moments of comedy which are frequently interwoven with and in the end heighten the tragedy. People who knew Lorca have observed that throughout his life he retained an impish, childlike humour and that even in the darkest moments his laughter was liable to burst through. See, for example, Ian Gibson, *Federico García Lorca: A Life*.

40 *It's nothing. Don't go*: see p. 81, note, 'a lively interplay of figures'. The conflict in the Bride is brilliantly suggested by the way in which she reacts, first to the two young girls, then to the Bridegroom when he embraces her from behind. Her impulsive 'Don't' at that moment reveals, of course, that she thinks he is Leonardo, and when just afterwards she implores the Bridegroom not to leave her, we see very clearly her fear of Leonardo's power over her and her inability to resist it. But Lorca's skill as a dramatist lies too in the fact that while the Bride's predicament is made clear to us, the audience, it is concealed from the characters on the stage.

It's as if someone's struck me on the head: see the Mother's reaction in Act One, Scene One, to the Bride's name: 'But even so, when I mention her name, it's as if they were pounding my head with a stone.' Just as the Mother fears for her son's and her own future, so the Bride senses, in a physical manner, that something terrible is about to happen. The sense of fate and inevitable doom is palpable in this and Lorca's other tragedies, as real to the characters as the food they eat. In addition, the lines serve to link the Mother and the Bride, just as they are linked in the play in many other ways.

42 *I'll always do what you want me to*: see p. 73, note, 'A kind of lump in my throat'. In the course of Act Two there are signs that the Bridegroom is more manly and assertive, for he flirts with the Servant, embraces the Bride in public and shows every sign of wanting to accompany her to the bedroom. On the other hand, he continues to be submissive to his mother, as in this instance, and is completely different from Leonardo, whose passionate outbursts we have observed in the earlier part of the act.

A lot of noise and guitars: in terms of its theatricality the end of the act is very effective indeed. Earlier we have been presented with *a lively interplay of figures*. That sense of animation and celebration continues now with the dance that is announced, but at the same time it is interwoven with the increasingly agitated exits and entrances of those who are looking for the Bride. The positive and joyous thrust of the wedding celebrations is thus offset by elements of discord – a juxtaposition of opposites which is characteristic of the play as a whole.

On horseback: See p. 70, note, 'as if he's come . . .' There is an informative study of the horse in the works of Lorca by Rafael Martínez Nadal, *Lorca's 'The Public': A Study of his Unfinished Play (El Público) and of Love and Death in the Work of Federico García Lorca*, pp. 185–217. The horse on which the Bride escapes with Leonardo signifies their unbridled passion, their instinctive response to their situation, but often in Lorca's work the horse has connotations of fate and death, as in the poem 'Dialogue of Amargo, the Bitter One', in which the young man, El Amargo, meets the mysterious rider who is in fact Death.

43 *A plant from a wicked mother*: see p. 73, note, 'She's like my wife . . .'; and p. 78, note, 'if my mother were to call me'.

Go! After them!: although the Bridegroom has already indicated his intention to pursue the runaway lovers, it is probably his mother's words which clinch the matter. She is herself torn in different directions – fearful for her son as well as enraged by the events that have taken place – but now it is offended honour which matters and the vengeance which offended honour demands. See p. 76, note 'I'm a man of honour'. Such is the dishonour inflicted on the Bridegroom by Leonardo's abduction of the Bride that his offence can only be eradicated by his death.

Act Three

Scene One

44 *A forest*: the stage setting here is intended to be not naturalistic but stylised, an appropriate background to the stylised figures of the Woodcutters, Moon and Death, and matched too to the highly stylised lighting that is used throughout the scene. Lorca had already rehearsed the scene to some extent in *When Five Years Pass*, completed in 1931, for the third act contains in its two scenes figures in black which pass amongst tree trunks and three cardplayers who pay a final fatal visit to the play's protagonist. In *Blood Wedding* Lorca's debt to Greek drama should be noted too, for the three Woodcutters suggest the Greek Fates on the one hand and the Chorus of Greek tragic drama on the other.

Everyone can live in it: the First Woodcutter's words echo Lorca's longing for a society far more tolerant than that in which he lived and in which his own homosexuality, no less than the illicit passion of couples like the Bride and Leonardo, would be more readily accepted.

the blood was strongest: blood is alluded to on many occasions in the play and in different ways. On the one hand, blood is life and spilt blood death. On the other, blood is heredity, good or bad in its effects. But blood is also passion. When the First Woodcutter observes that 'the blood was strongest' and continues 'You have to follow the blood's path', he is referring to passion and instinct, and also to heredity, which is inescapable, and therefore to fate. The various meanings of 'blood' come together in the Woodcutters' dialogue, just as the various threads of the action fuse in the final act.

45 *like two empty pitchers*: a fine example of a very concrete simile, drawn from rural life, which is wonderfully evocative. See p. 64, note, 'the knife'. A comparison may be made here

with *Yerma*, Act Two, Scene Two, where Yerma returns to the house with two pitchers brimming with water, an ironic contrast to her own infertility and sense of emptiness.

A tree with forty branches: while the reference may be to a specific tree, it clearly has broader implications, given the fate-like presence of the Woodcutters and the links established throughout the play between branches and families. See p. 81, note, 'Whole branches of families'.

46 *The* MOON *is a young woodcutter with a white face*: at this point the action moves onto a different plane and the mysterious forces of fate and destiny, which in Acts One and Two remain unseen, now acquire a physical form. For William I. Oliver ('The Trouble with Lorca', *Modern Drama*, 7 (1964), p. 6), the symbolism of Act Three is a discordant element: 'Lorca in no way justifies a departure from the heightened realism of the first two acts of the play. His figures and his "basic" plot are capable of forcefully expressing everything encompassed in this play without aid of such allegorical beings as the Moon and Death . . .'. For Lorca himself the transition from human to non-human figures, from a 'realistic' to a 'poetic' level, was the best part of the play. There can be no doubt that he was right, but the point should be made that the transition is not as abrupt as has sometimes been suggested, for in such moments as the lullaby of Act One, Scene Two, the presence of dark forces is strongly felt.

Round swan on the river: the circle of the moon, reflected in the river, resembles a swan, and high in the sky, seen amongst the spires of cathedrals, is like an eye. The way in which one object is seen in terms of another links Lorca's vision and poetic method with that of the seventeenth-century poet, Luis de Góngora, on whose poetry Lorca gave his famous lecture in 1927, *The Poetic Image in Don Luis de Góngora.*

The moon places a knife: the silvery light of the moon is like the gleam of a knife. We are reminded here of the ominous implications of the lullaby in Act One, Scene Two, where the reflection of the water in the horse's eye suggests a broken dagger.

Seek the crest of fire: the moon, like the cold ashes of a fire, would presumably wish to be the sun as it rises to flood mountains and streets with warmth and light. Lorca's personification of the moon as a young man frozen with cold is quite brilliant in the sense that it allows us to feel sympathy for this icy agent of death.

On its back of jasper: the reference is less to colour than to the smooth, cold surface of snow when frozen.

47 *The torn flight of their screams*: this is a magnificent metaphor to suggest the way in which the cries of the two men will fly through the air like panic-stricken birds.

48 *white linen*: the winding-sheets which are in Spain traditionally kept in chests.

The intense blue light returns: blue lighting is used here and elsewhere in Lorca's plays to suggest the imminence of death. In a very effective scene in *When Five Years Pass*, a dead child and a dead cat appear on stage and the scene takes place in '*the blue light of storm*'. Similarly, the stage direction for Act Three of *The House of Bernarda Alba* suggests '*white walls lightly touched by blue*', pointing to the fact that death is not far away.

hard, and double-edged: the whole of Nature seems to be coming to the assistance of the Moon and Death. The wind itself suddenly has the sharpness, coldness and penetration of a knife. This is a good example of how simple yet effective Lorca's images are.

49 *And it's got such strength*: as we have seen, Acts One and Two presented the Bridegroom as a rather passive character, a complete contrast to the assertively masculine Leonardo. Act Three demands that he be a worthy opponent for him, and he duly becomes this by taking upon himself the avenging role demanded by his family. It is not so much a change of character, rather the assumption of a role imposed upon him.

50 *Oh rising death!*: the ten lines chanted by the Woodcutters are now full of anguish, preparing the way for the tragedy and lamentation that are to follow. At the beginning of the act, the mood was different, even hopeful at times, but now all three are one in their acceptance of inevitable death.

51 *With your teeth*: for the first time in the play the human characters are made to speak their lines in the heightened form of poetry. Previously, in Acts One and Two, poetry has consisted entirely of songs.

the blue branches: the metaphor creates a link between Man and Nature on the one hand, and connects too, of course, with the idea of the family-tree that occurs from time to time in the play. On the first point, the entwined limbs of the lovers are echoed in the twisting branches of the trees which surround them.

52 *Turned my red blood black*: just as longing for Leonardo has turned the Bride's blood putrid, so the thought of her coming marriage has driven him mad. The allusion to black blood connects too with the ominously black water from which the horse of the lullaby refuses to drink.

The fault belongs to the earth: his assertion that he has no freedom of choice connects with the statement of the Third Woodcutter earlier in the act: 'You have to follow your instinct.' The whole of the scene consists of the conflict between the Bride and Leonardo and of the struggle within them between the course of action they have attempted to take – avoiding each other – and that imposed upon them by their inescapable mutual attraction, between their feelings of guilt and their desperate longing.

54 *Nails of moonlight*: presumably the light that filters through the trees, creating a patterned effect on the two bodies. The image of nails driven through and joining the lovers suggests inseparability but also, of course, the Crucifixion or, at the very least, martyrdom. In 'The Gypsy Nun', one of the poems of *Gypsy Ballads*, the suffering and bitterness of the young woman, condemned to a life in the convent, are embodied in five grapefruit, while alongside them are five nasturtiums, commonly known in Spanish as 'the wounds of Christ'. In other words, the Bride, Leonardo, the gypsy nun and many other Lorcan figures are associated with Christ and the persecution inflicted upon him.

And thorns stuck in my head: the allusion reinforces the crucifixion motif but it links too with earlier references to thorns. In Act Two, Scene One, Leonardo refers bitterly to the pain inflicted on him by the thought that the Bride abandoned him for money. At the end of the same scene Leonardo's wife compares the hostility she sees in his eyes to thorns. The image is yet another example of Lorca's ability to suggest emotional states by means of tangible objects, often selected from the natural world. The effect is immediate and telling.

Scene Two

55 *anything that creates perspective*: once more the emphasis is on stylisation. The setting, stripped of shadow and sense of perspective, becomes timeless. It is interesting to note how the 'white room with arches and thick walls' became three years later the setting for Act One of *The House of Bernarda Alba*. Clearly, Lorca had in mind for this last scene the interior of small Spanish churches with their white walls, churches which he knew and in which he had often seen widows, dressed in black, praying for their loved ones. But it was his method to take something that was real and which he knew well and to raise it to a more symbolic and suggestive plane. The whiteness here suggests less spirituality than the emptiness of death, the white corpse from which the blood has been drained.

Two GIRLS *dressed in dark blue*: on the one hand the two girls and the little girl are village girls who chat about the wedding as they spin; on the other they are the Fates of Greek mythology, Clotho, Lachesis and Atropos, unwinding the thread of life. The thread of red wool is reminiscent not only of blood but also of the network of veins referred to earlier by the bride.

At ten finishing: this is the kind of song which village women at their work would be likely to sing, but Lorca relates every line of it to the events concerning the Bride, the Bridegroom and Leonardo, thereby intensifying the feeling of fate that hangs heavily over the play's conclusion. Thus, when the question is asked of the wool, 'Oh wool, oh wool, / What will you say?', the answer is chilling: 'The lover's dumb, / The young man red. / On the silent shore / I saw them spread.' And the mood is, of course, intensified too by the monotonous rhythm of the lines, as though they are tolling for the Bridegroom and Leonardo.

And myrtle's ache: the myrtle-tree or shrub is particularly associated with southern Europe. The colour of the flower of the myrtle-tree is white or pink, and Lorca is evidently using the pink flower here as a metaphor for flesh or blood.

56 *And the sheets marble-clear*: the sheets are like a cold, white slab containing the bloodless corpses.

Brave and alone in your house: the image evoked by the Mother-in-Law is precisely that of the Mother at the beginning of the play. We recall her words to her son: '. . . I'll be left alone. Only you are left to me now and I'm sorry to see you going.' With the death of Leonardo, the Wife is, of course, the widow that the Mother became with the murder of her husband, and with the death of the Bridegroom the Bride's fate is the same – three women sharing an identical fate. The Mother-in-Law's allusion to nailing up the windows anticipates the situation in *The House of Bernarda Alba* when, on the death of her husband, the tradition-obsessed Bernarda imposes on the household a period of mourning in which the windows will be shuttered and the doors closed.

57 *Place a cross of ash*: ash contrasts vividly with the flame, i.e. the passion, that precedes it, and is also a traditional image for death. There is an incident in Luis Buñuel's film, *Viridiana*, when the sleepwalking girl pours ashes on her uncle's marriage bed, which is a perfect illustration of the meaning of Lorca's lines.

two rushing streams: what could be simpler to suggest the vitality of young manhood and the stillness of a pool to evoke its sudden ending? Like fire and blood, water is an image which in Lorca's work has many meanings, depending on the context in which it is used.

58 *Two fistfuls of frozen snow*: yet another example of a very simple metaphor, yet what could suggest the teeth of a dead man better than this, and what could be more appropriate to express eyes that are now dull and lifeless than the circular form of a dead or damaged flower? Lorca's instinct for the telling yet simple image is remarkable.

dirty sand: earlier in the play the Bridegroom has been associated with yellow, an image of youth and vitality. See p. 64, note, 'Room painted yellow'. In the wedding scene, Act Two, Scene One, he is alluded to by the First Girl: 'The bridegroom / Is a golden flower.' Now, in death, the golden flower of youth is tarnished, the body itself dirtied by the mud of the stream where it lay. The duality of yellow in Lorca's work is well illustrated by this example.

59 *from the soles of my feet*: a good example of that relationship between Man and Nature that is such a central feature of Lorca's writing. A similar example can be found in *Yerma*, Act One, Scene One, when Yerma describes to a neighbour, Maria, how, in her desire to have a child, she goes out at night and places her bare feet on the earth, feeling instinctively that Nature will fill her body with its own creative energy.

not a graveyard: a bed of earth: from the beginning of this last act the stylisation and universalisation of the action through setting and image are constant, humans and landscape merge more and more, and the play moves progressively onto the level of myth.

I don't want them to see me so poor: even in the moments of greatest anguish, a concern with appearance and public opinion is still evident. In similar fashion the grief of Bernarda Alba and her children, first for a husband and a father, later for a daughter and a sister, must not be unseemly.

60 *Where is his name?*: as far as the Mother is concerned, the Bride's behaviour has irredeemably stained her son's name and reputation in the eyes of others.

I want her to know that I'm clean: the Bride asserts, and there is no reason to disbelieve what she says, that she is still a virgin. But this does not alter the fact that she ran off with Leonardo and it will not stop people from pondering on what may have taken place between them. In short, her assertion of virginity does not restore the Bridegroom's honour.

I was a woman burning: see p. 74, note, 'in this heat', and p. 76, note, 'To keep quiet and burn'. For the Bride the Bridegroom was, as she now observes, 'a tiny drop of water', insufficient to quench her sexual thirst. Leonardo, in contrast, was 'a dark river', which not only quenched her thirst but swept her helplessly away. On the one hand he fills her with fire, on the other only he can satisfy her longing, leaving 'frost on the wounds of this poor, withered woman'. While the Bride cannot resist Leonardo's inexplicable attraction, she is not unaware of the danger which that attraction represents, just as the horse of the lullaby is drawn to drink from the stream but senses a danger at the spot where 'the water's oh so black'. By the time we reach the end of the play, the significance of the lullaby in terms of its menacing implications and links with the rest of the action is very clear.

61 *Blessed be the wheat*: we recall the Mother's words in the opening scene: 'That's what I like. Men to be men; wheat wheat.'

a frozen heap of snow: see p. 89, note, 'Two fistfuls of frozen snow'. There is also the point that the metaphor of frozen snow is appropriate to a man who in life had the vibrant vitality of flowing water.

Sunflower for your mother: another example of yellow, with its associations of vitality, and it links, of course, with the earlier allusion to the Bridegroom as 'the golden flower'.

62 *bitter oleander*: the oleander bush, which produces deep pink or red flowers, is a common enough sight in Spain and other Mediterranean countries. The leaves and flowers have a bitter taste and are associated in Andalusia with marital infidelity, as is the case here. As we have seen, the American translation by José Weissberger, presented in New York in 1935, bore the title *Bitter Oleander*. Quite apart from being meaningless to all but those familiar with Spanish tradition, it is a title which has none of the paradox and irony of *Blood Wedding*.

Neighbours: with a knife: the ending of the play has aroused considerable differences of opinion. William I. Oliver ('The Trouble with Lorca', *Modern Drama*, 7 (1964), pp. 13–15), is highly critical of this final lament: '. . . having ended *Blood Wedding* with the Mother's moving and shocking confession, her surrender of pride, Lorca gave in to the suggestion of Margarita Xirgu and added the sensational but thematically misleading section about "With a knife, a little knife . . ." etc. This last section shows us a group of women sitting and making great noises of agony. How unlike a similar ending in *Riders to the Sea* in which the endless struggle of life is actually affirmed. However, this is not the way with Lorcan tragic endings. They all end in a great clap of negative despair . . .'. Presumably, Oliver saw the enthusiastic reaction of the Madrid audiences of 1933 as a justification of his own view: commercialism triumphant over art. However, that reaction accorded with the opinion of many of Lorca's intelligent friends, who were deeply moved by the ending. Oliver's comments are clearly self-contradictory, for he suggests on the one hand that Lorca's endings are full of 'negative despair', and on the other that this particular ending, concentrating on the women's grief, was really written on the suggestion of someone else. Neither is it, as Oliver suggests, 'thematically misleading', for the knife, the instrument of fate, has been suspended over the characters from the play's opening sequence. A final emphasis on it gives the play both a tight thematic coherence and a circular structure which suggests the inescapable, inevitable nature of Fate.

Fish without scales or river: the silver blade of the knife has the glint and the smoothness of a fish. The image is strongly reminiscent of the seventeenth-century dramatist, Calderón de la Barca, some of whose plays Lorca had directed with his touring theatre company, La Barraca. Calderón's complex imagery is characterised by a system of correspondences in which an object belonging to one of the elements of earth, air, fire and water, is described in terms of another: a serpent as a stream, a star as a flower, a mountain as an ocean, etc. Lorca's image is clearly drawn from the opening lines of Calderón's *Life is a Dream*, where Rosaura, thrown from her horse, describes its wildness in a flurry of images: 'Or lightning, perhaps, without / Its flash of light, or scale-less fish . . .'. In turn, Calderón's imagery owed much to that of the contemporary poet, Luis de Góngora, who for Lorca and other poets of his generation, became a cult figure.

63 *And lips turned yellow*: see p. 64, note, 'Room painted yellow'.

Leonardo and the Wife
(Act One, Scene Two)

The Mother meets the Bride
(Act One, Scene Three)

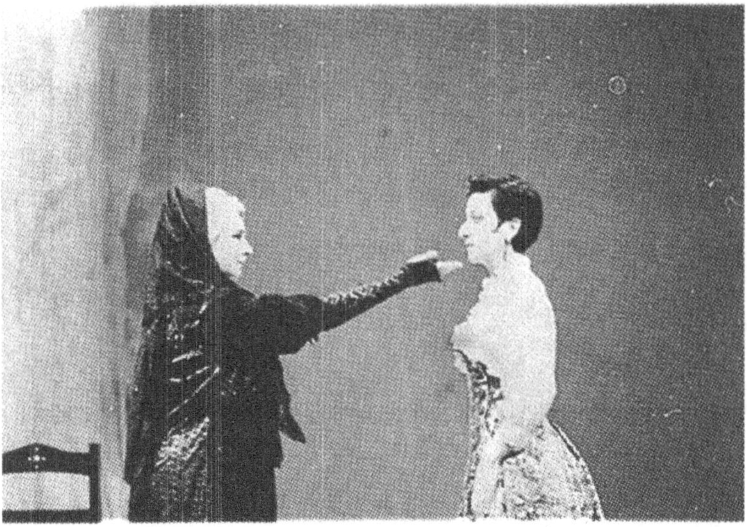

The Bridegroom and the Mother
(Act One, Scene Three)

The Bride prepares to get dressed for the wedding
(Act Two, Scene One)

The guests arrive for the wedding
(Act Two, Scene One)

The Bride at the wedding reception
(Act Two, Scene Two)

Leonardo and the Bride in flight
(Act Three, Scene One)

Death and the Moon in the forest
(Act Three, Scene One)

The Mother and the Bride confront each other
(Act Three, Scene Two)

Questions for Further Study

1. How does the play evoke the places in which the Bridegroom and the Bride live? What do we learn about their family backgrounds and how does the feud between the families of the Bridegroom and Leonardo affect the action of the play?
2. How does the title of *Blood Wedding* relate to the events that take place?
3. Is Lorca critical of the social values of *Blood Wedding*?
4. Can any of the principal characters of *Blood Wedding* be described as sympathetic?
5. 'Passion and frustration are always linked in Lorca's plays.' Relate this statement to *Blood Wedding*.
6. Discuss the importance of fate in *Blood Wedding*.
7. To what extent can *Blood Wedding* be regarded as a tragedy?
8. Assess the importance of symbolism and imagery in *Blood Wedding*.
9. Which of the characters of *Blood Wedding* appeals to you most and why?
10. '*Blood Wedding* is set in rural Spain but its relevance is universal.' Discuss.
11. 'Realism was never part of Lorca's approach to writing plays.' Do you agree, with reference to *Blood Wedding*?
12. Examine the importance of colour in *Blood Wedding*.
13. Do you think that the contrast in style between Act Three and the first two acts of *Blood Wedding* is too great?
14. Assess the importance of songs and choral passages in *Blood Wedding*.
15. Do you consider the characters of *Blood Wedding* to be too one-dimensional?
16. If you were staging *Blood Wedding*, how would you approach the task?
17. '*Blood Wedding* illustrates perfectly Lorca's concept of

total theatre.' What does this statement mean?

18. 'The acting style demanded by *Blood Wedding* is very different from that to which British actors are accustomed.' Do you agree?
19. Choose a scene from *Blood Wedding* and assess its main characteristics.
20. Do you believe that a production of *Blood Wedding* should preserve as many of its Spanish characteristics as possible? If so, describe what they should be.

GWYNNE EDWARDS is a specialist in Spanish theatre and cinema, until recently teaching at the University of Aberystwyth. His books include: *Lorca: The Theatre Beneath the Sand*; *Lorca: Living in the Theatre*; *Dramatists in Perspective: Spanish Theatre in the Twentieth Century*; *The Discreet Art of Luis Buñuel*; *A Companion to Luis Buñuel*; and *Almodóvar: Labyrinths of Passion*. He has also translated and adapted more than forty plays from Spanish, French and Italian, many of which have been staged at major theatres in Britain and the United States. He has published three collections of Lorca plays with Methuen Drama, together with student editions of *The House of Bernarda Alba* and *Yerma* and also collections of seventeenth-century Spanish and contemporary Spanish American plays. Other recent works include two plays adapted from the correspondence and prose writings of Dylan Thomas.

Bloomsbury Methuen Drama Student Editions

Jean Anouilh *Antigone* • John Arden *Serjeant Musgrave's Dance* Alan Ayckbourn *Confusions* • Aphra Behn *The Rover* • Edward Bond *Lear* • *Saved* • Bertolt Brecht *The Caucasian Chalk Circle* • *Fear and Misery in the Third Reich* • *The Good Person of Szechwan* • *Life of Galileo* • *Mother Courage and her Children* • *The Resistible Rise of Arturo Ui* • *The Threepenny Opera* • Anton Chekhov *The Cherry Orchard* • *The Seagull* • *Three Sisters* • *Uncle Vanya* • Caryl Churchill *Serious Money* • *Top Girls* • Shelagh Delaney *A Taste of Honey* • Euripides *Elektra* • *Medea* • Dario Fo *Accidental Death of an Anarchist* • Michael Frayn *Copenhagen* • John Galsworthy *Strife* • Nikolai Gogol *The Government Inspector* • Robert Holman *Across Oka* • Henrik Ibsen *A Doll's House* • *Ghosts* • *Hedda Gabler* • Charlotte Keatley *My Mother Said I Never Should* • Bernard Kops *Dreams of Anne Frank* • Federico García Lorca *Blood Wedding* • *Doña Rosita the Spinster* (bilingual edition) • *The House of Bernarda Alba* • (bilingual edition) • *Yerma* (bilingual edition) • David Mamet *Glengarry Glen Ross* • *Oleanna* • Patrick Marber *Closer* • John Marston *Malcontent* • Martin McDonagh *The Lieutenant of Inishmore* • Joe Orton *Loot* • Luigi Pirandello *Six Characters in Search of an Author* • Mark Ravenhill *Shopping and F***ing* • Willy Russell *Blood Brothers* • *Educating Rita* • Sophocles *Antigone* • *Oedipus the King* • Wole Soyinka *Death and the King's Horseman* • Shelagh Stephenson *The Memory of Water* • August Strindberg *Miss Julie* • J. M. Synge *The Playboy of the Western World* • Theatre Workshop *Oh What a Lovely War* Timberlake Wertenbaker *Our Country's Good* • Arnold Wesker *The Merchant* • Oscar Wilde *The Importance of Being Earnest* • Tennessee Williams *A Streetcar Named Desire* • *The Glass Menagerie*